Fame 101

Powerful Personal Branding & Publicity for Amazing Success

www.dallasjessup.com

Publicity & Branding Secrets of the Power Elite
Anyone Can Use To Become the Celebrity
Alpha Brand of Their Profession

SUTTON HART PRESS

www.suttonhart.com

Fame 101

Powerful Personal Branding & Publicity for Amazing Success

Jay Jessup & Maggie Jessup

SUTTON HART PRESS

www.suttonhart.com

Fame 101 is Published by Sutton Hart Press LLC

P.O. 5647 Vancouver, Washington 98668

Inquiries – information@suttonhart.com

Website - www.suttonhart.com

Authors' Website - www.platformstrategy.com

First printing January, 2010

Copyright 2013 by Jay Jessup

All rights reserved.

ISBN 978-0-981-98883-2

LCCN 2009936889

Library of Congress Cataloging-In-Publication Data Has Been Applied For

Printed in the United States of America

Media & Reviewer Contact – maggie@platformstrategy.com

Cover design: Maria Elias

Copy editor: Anabel Wirth

Layout design: Jason Enterline

Cover image: Getty images

No part of this publication may be reproduced, stored in, or included in a retrieval system, or transmitted in any form without the prior written consent of the publisher. Your support of the authors' rights is appreciated.

DEDICATION

For our daughter Dallas and our amazing friends.
- Vancouver, Washington

CONTENTS

THE FAME FORMULA

THE CELEBRITY NEXT DOOR

YOUR FAME FOUNDATION

EVERYONE LOVES AN AUTHOR

YOU DOT COM

CREATE A POWERFUL PRESENCE

FAME FUEL

SUCCESSFUL PERSONAL BRANDS

LEVERAGING FAME

FAME BARRIERS

FAME FOR LIFE

PREVIEW OF
FAME 101

Fame is America's most powerful force and anyone can harness it with compelling personal branding. Fame 101 is the playbook for extraordinary professional success. The rewards are wealth, power, access, recognition, and other tools for an extraordinary life.

Every profession has its super successful celebrities and *FAME 101* shows the reader exactly how to become one of them. These are lawyers who attract high-value clients, brokers who seemingly fall into high-dollar deals, doctors who are high-visibility media magnets, as well as players in many newly-celebrified fields.

Meet cooks who brand themselves into celebrity chef'dom with television shows and big book deals, political unknowns who explode onto the national stage, authors who brand a path from the kitchen table to best seller lists and movie deals, and other everyday people who join society's elite.

Personal branding pioneers Jay and Maggie Jessup take the reader backstage through Fame's history from the early Hollywood star-making machine through to today's Internet celebrities. They demonstrate that the successes of JFK, Mother Theresa, Martha Stewart, President Obama, Rachael Ray, and the leading voice of every profession are all created with the very same strategy – the Fame Formula.

Fame 101 is a comprehensive guide to creating a very visible powerful personal brand with messaging, image, presence, book deals, strategic websites, social media, speaking engagements, articles, publicity, and other platform elements used by the power elite.

It is empowering to walk into a room full of strangers where everyone already knows who you are and they are excited about meeting you. Professional fame gives you that; in every room – every time. Fame separates you from the crowd – you become a celebrity in your field; it lets you live and work in a place of power.

***Fame 101* is the ultimate guide to personal branding, publicity, professional celebrity, and the other components of Fame for anyone wanting to increase their visibility, capture the power of a compelling personal brand, and monetize the results.**

Jay Jessup creates and manages alpha celebrities in many professions as co-founder of Platform Strategy, a publicity & branding boutique. A featured Mensa speaker, a guest on business television including CNN's *Moneyline* and NPR's *Marketplace*, Jay is a graduate of USC and Hastings College of Law. His prior work was in the technology, publishing, and entertainment sectors.

Maggie Jessup builds celebrities in every field with a unique mix of publicity, brand strategy, and marketing. Her clients appear regularly on CNN, MSNBC, Fox, and moar other outlets as well as in USA Today, Forbes, InTouch Weekly and scores of similarly varied publications. Prior to co-founding Platform Strategy she was a reporter at the Atlanta Journal Constitution and the Houston Chronicle.

INTRODUCTION

Fame is the key to an amazing life and career. Anyone can have it if they are willing to work smart and hard. It's the secret of rock stars, award winning actors, successful politicians, best selling authors, business titans, celebrity chefs, notable scientists, very visible doctors, superstar lawyers, the home remodelers on prime time television, and the leading voice of your own industry. You can have it too – Fame 101 will show you how.

What would it be like to live your life to its maximum potential; an all-dreams-realized existence? For some, this would mean a really big income, for others it might mean the opportunity and resources to make a big impact in the world. How about an exciting lifestyle, an exhilarating professional life, or the freedom and independence to live pretty much as you please? In essence, to leap past the "uphill battle" part of life.

Only a small percentage of people get to live like this but we have discovered that pretty much everyone has within themselves the opportunity to capture their own potential and catapult themselves to live their dream life. Money, access, power, freedom, security, credibility, respect, free time – Fame 101 is a blueprint for having all of those things in your life.

We have created a replicable process that anyone can use to become their best professional self and live a maximized life; whatever that might mean to them. The process harnesses possibly the most powerful force in society to empower you to live up to your best professional imaginings. We call this force Fame, our process the Fame Formula, and you can use this formula to win a life and career beyond your dreams.

How do we know our Fame Formula works? We use it successfully every day. You see, we are in the fame business. We create it, amplify it, monetize it, nurture it, and maximize it for clients of our personal brand strategy boutique. In the last ten years we have worked with many people you know from the Who's Who list and even more from the Who's Next list of personal brands that are just launching.

Our interest in Fame started many years ago when I was a rainmaker for a global financial consulting firm and Maggie was an investigative reporter for a Top 20 newspaper. Our insanely busy lifestyles connected us socially and professionally with celebrity CEOs, quite-visible royals, up-and-coming politicians, technology gurus, evangelists, some rock legends, well known journalists, cool authors, and others who live in the top one percent of society.

We had a simultaneous dinner table epiphany when I was telling Maggie about my quirky business trip where in 72 hours I dined at a Texas barbeque stand with a Lord and Lady, had sushi with a rock legend, met with a phenomenally well known evangelist, and connected with a first-time author whose book had just hit the New York Times best seller list.

This same week Maggie interviewed an almost-president Republican Congressman, a sports legend, a quirky billionaire, and heard from the publicity team at the head office of one of the world's largest religions. My business associates were begging for personal details of my meetings while Maggie's editors clamored for inside-info on her contacts.

We joked about how otherwise normal people were somehow entranced by the celebrity types we met regularly and we noted they lost all pretense of cool at the hope that they too, through us, might get to meet a rock star or go backstage at a nationally televised revival. The idea of a photo op with a best selling author or member of the royal court was an immense personal aspiration.

As we considered what it was that made each of these notables so desirable a "get" for business deals, lunches or photo opportunities, it occurred to us that all of these people had some sort of X factor that made them celebrities. And suddenly we had our "Aha" moment: each of these people, although in very diverse categories, had created a powerful X factor in the very same way.

There was no difference in the X factor of the rock star, the evangelist, the sports legend, the author, or the Congressman. They were masters of personal branding (although this term didn't yet exist) and they knew the power of publicity. It was that combination that put them among society's elite and kept them there. Our dinner table discovery of this powerhouse strategy changed in an instant the course of our lives and careers.

If you're having a hard time believing the strategic commonalities of the evangelist that multiple generations of Americans have revered, the well-spoken charismatic Congressman from a southern state, a best selling author and other big personal brands, consider their common business and life models.

Rock stars are doing their professional thing on stage; so too the evangelist. Authors get successful by capturing the media stage with an Oprah appearance, while politicians commonly leap onto any stage. Rock stars want to build a fan base and capture the names of their fans so they can connect directly. Faith based personal brands want to build their flock and gather their own list so they too can connect directly. Politicians use voter lists to spread their message and keep meticulous track of their donors as do evangelists. Authors want to know who reads their books, as do their publishers. You see where we're going with all this.

We are now getting into the many ways people brand themselves and become celebrities in their field which is a subject covered in detail throughout Fame 101 but for now please accept what we discovered on that day – that the top people of every field are doing the very same thing when it comes to joining society's elite; it's personal branding with killer publicity. The effort makes them visible and attracts people, opportunities, and money to them.

In the weeks that followed our moment of realization we looked at countless personal brands in every field. Our thought was that you could step out of the world of traditional celebrity fame and use the very same tools, techniques, technology, and strategy used by the power elite to capture celebrity in effectively any field.

Could a school teacher become a big national brand? Could an everyday lawyer capture national media attention and use it to create her own powerful personal brand? What about a surgeon, a real estate broker, a cook, or even a gardener? It seemed to us the same elements could work for each of these and pretty much anyone else – it was just a formula.

It was our belief that the common elements could be learned and applied. The traditionally famous all had very well-defined roles in society, from JFK to Michael Jordan or Larry King. Each celebrity had a foundational message, great messaging to support that message, and great communication skills from one-on-one to speaking on stage in front of thousands or on television speaking to millions.

Most had well-publicized books, whether they wrote them or had them written. All were regularly in the media. Every one of them looked and acted the role they had defined for themselves with no inconsistencies. Nearly everyone we looked at with even marginal celebrity status had found a way to make a living, and sometimes gather great wealth, in similar ways by leveraging their powerful personal brands.

They had learned to use their brand to win votes, sell books, gather the faithful, build companies, gain support for their non profit, get film roles, and be more successful in their professional lives than their non personal-brand-savvy competitors. Every one of the celebrities we looked at were just normal people who identified something remarkable about themselves and defined their role and consistently built their brand – they also had the common element of a keen interest in and facility with publicity.

These were the origins of our company, Platform Strategy, and ultimately this book. We discovered a fame formula and have in the following years applied it to the careers of business leaders, medical professionals, attorneys, shamans, pastors, conservatives, liberals, entertainers, actors, tech gurus, artists, writers, professional speakers and others with amazing results.

What we do and what you can learn to do for yourself with this book, is to identify what is remarkable and unique about a person, create an authentic role for them, train them with a speech coach, media coach and other professionals, get a book deal, harness social media outlets, attract local, regional, and national media, build a substantial online presence, and with this foundation, launch toward the top one percent of any profession.

You're likely seeing that creating and monetizing fame is a lot of work; building a foundation is more than a half dozen independent tasks and the monetary return on the time and money you invest doesn't start happening for six months or even a year. On the other hand, imagine yourself twelve months from now, with an exceptional personal brand, a book, frequent media appearances, and an income in the mid six figure range or even higher.

So yes, professional fame can bring you money, security, access, power, credibility, freedom, and much more. Fame can be taught, it can be learned, and you can win it for yourself. Have you got the courage to step up and capture an amazing life and career? If yes, we wrote this book for you. Let it be your guidebook. Enjoy Fame 101 and let us know how you do. We'll be watching for you in the media.

- Jay Jessup

WHAT IS FAME?
THE MOST POWERFUL FORCE IN OUR OPRAHFIED UNIVERSE

. . . .

"Fame is very big and very visible professional success. It is the key to the good side of life's velvet ropes. For those who win it, society will grant them wealth, power, access, recognition, and other tools to live an extraordinary life." —Jay Jessup

. . . .

FAME CONVERTS HARD WORK INTO SUCCESS

Are you giving 100% in your career and in your life? Perhaps you are but often that's just not enough. A less-talented actor gets picked for your perfect role, an opposing candidate with half your vision wins the election in a landslide, or the lawyer next door gets the high dollar clients although his courtroom skills pale in comparison to your own. Guess which of these people knows about the fame formula – here's a hint: it isn't you.

Our parents and teachers tell us that it takes hard work to become a big success; others speculate that some people are born with natural talents that assure a rise to the top of their field. In our experience, based upon working with hundreds of personal brands over more than a decade, it's not hard work or talent that puts people in the top one percent of their profession.

Don't misunderstand us; hard work makes a big difference in your life as does natural talent but the distinction between the talented hard workers and the immensely successful is either an intuitive or learned understanding of what we call the Fame Formula. It's the secret known to winning candidates, bestselling authors, top actors, corporate-types with meteoric careers, thriving consultants, business owners with a seemingly golden touch and the great news is it can work for anyone.

Fame might be a misnomer as many people confuse it with Celebrity. Paris Hilton has celebrity, John Travolta has fame. Lindsay Lohan has celebrity, Barrack Obama has fame. The faces on the covers of magazines at the supermarket checkout aisle are of celebrities; celebrity is about paparazzi and selling baby pictures for millions. Fame is professional success enjoyed by society's true elite; it's what you get when you apply the fame formula.

Our definition of fame is very big and very visible personal success. Some people are on life's stage, while others merely play background – you're likely reading this book because you want to be the one on stage or at least to see if it's an option for your life. Here's the headline - anyone can use the fame formula to capture the spotlight and turn that visibility into unprecedented professional and personal success.

Even better news, you can use that spotlight to create success beyond all imagining and you can do it in any field. This is what fame is all about and we have discovered the formula that makes it all happen. You'll find that formula detailed in another chapter but first we need to understand this concept that we call fame.

WHAT IS FAME?

Fame is our society's most powerful force; celebrities, those that have it, are the super elite of our culture. If you doubt the concept, drop in on any DC cocktail party and watch Nobel Prize winners, powerful Congressmen and Fortune 500 board chairs become blithering idiots when introduced to Brad Pitt or Tiger Woods or John Grisham. Fame is more than sex appeal, it's more than charisma and it's not just for rock stars. Quite simply it is raw power of the most exciting sort.

Fame doesn't lend itself to simple definition but you can explain it by example:

- Fame is why the latest Diet Doctor gets 10 times more press than the world's most promising stem cell scientist.
- Fame is why the first photos of J- Lo's baby sold for millions and pics of your child are languishing on Ebay with a one dollar bid.
- Fame is why Paula Deen could run for Congress in Georgia and probably win.
- Fame is why we pay attention to Paris Hilton, cleverly branded as America's party girl.

- Fame explains President Obama's election, Governor
  Terminator's second term and it's why the guy who graduated at
  the bottom of your law school class has a book deal, the very
  best clients, and is always on CNN.

We all know fame when we see it but perhaps we don't recognize exactly what it is; rather, we just know that the famous are somehow just a little bit better or at least more interesting than the rest of us. In essence, fame is that difference between us and them; defining that difference and learning their strategies and secrets is what this book is about.

The famous are actors on the world stage; they've developed their role and they know their audience. Fame isn't wealth, lots of people are rich but don't have the power fame delivers but many have discovered the path to wealth is much easier for the famous. It isn't breathtaking physical beauty although Jen, Angelina, Jessica and the rest have leveraged their genetic advantages into very public roles with adoring fans following their every move.

Of course, if you're the doc who enhanced Jen's figure, did Lisa's lips or helped Jessica lose those troubling extra pounds, you too can have fame. Oprah's best friend gets a book deal by branding herself as Oprah's Best Friend and even the bigoted cop, Mark Furman from the OJ Simpson trial, makes 7 figures as a television star. What are we all thinking? But, that's fame in action.

In our opinion, although some critics consider the celebrification of our society to be a dangerous cultural trend, we think they're wrong. We believe that fame, when used to benefit yourself and others in a positive manner, can be a good thing. Further, it provides entertainment in a sometimes troubling world, observing it in action is just plain fun and capturing it for yourself is the most phenomenal experience anyone could ever enjoy.

Whichever side of the Oprahfication debate you're on, our position is that we might as well accept the world the way it is and enjoy the characters we elevate to our society's highest positions. Even better, why don't we apply the fame formula to become one of them? We've discovered how you can make that happen and we share the tools, techniques, and technology in the following chapters.

Do you think these concepts don't apply to you because you're "just" a lawyer or "just" a garden guy? That fame is only for the entertainment folks? You couldn't be more wrong. Fame can be created and used in any field. We know it because we've created it for clients in more than 50 fields. Professional fame is partly show business and entertainment; you must accept and use this idea. Yes, we're saying that the local garden guy can be in the business of entertaining, not to be confused with the entertainment business.

If you're an attorney who wants to be a professional speaker, you must be entertaining because that's the business you're in when applying the fame formula. You'll need a head shot, demo reel and resume in the same format as an actor trying out for 90210 version 2.O. We talk about exactly how all this works throughout the book but it's important that you have the mindset that when you step into the fame arena, joining the elite of your field, you're in show business.

WHAT DO YOU GET? WEALTH, CREDIBILITY, RECOGNITION, AND FUN

Do you think this fame business is just too superficial? Consider this: the Dalai Lama and the Pope totally understand and use fame to spread the reach of their message; they just don't use it to get new Lamborghinis although they surely both have chauffeurs. If you still think fame is always shallow or phony skip ahead to the section entitled Mother Teresa's Publicity team in Chapter 2 and think about the number of lives she touched. The immensity of this small woman's power and reach would not have been possible without fame.

No one would ever call her a phony. She was able to geometrically expand her impact from the slums of India to a worldwide platform because she used this thing called fame. Maybe you saw this living saint on Larry King in one of her final appearances and she definitely didn't fly coach to get there.

Perhaps you're investing the time to read Fame 101 to understand how our world works but in my experience everyone at least wonders from time to time what it's all about and how some small difference in their personal history could have led to personal fame. Every one of us senses that there is some easier path for our own specific life; whatever road you're on, it becomes easier and much more impactful if you have fame. It's okay to want it. Let's look at what it delivers.

We've already seen that fame, or what some call celebrity status, is pure and simple power. It's why people stand behind ropes for hours on just the hope of seeing a second tier celebrity and it's why celebrity autographs can sell for $20,000 or even much more. So the first thing you get from fame is recognition and that really helps get things done.

What's cool is that you don't have to be Superbowl star Peyton Manning to be recognized. You can be the rock star teacher in the local high school because of your new book or a rock star pharmacist because of your syndicated blog. Recognition opens some amazing doors; many you never even knew were there. A curtain opens for the famous revealing life opportunities beyond the vision of the non-famous.

Fame also gives you immediate credibility, whether or not it's been yet fully earned. Society gives more credibility and value to the attorney who is the talking head expert on CNN than to the president of your local bar association. If she is a luncheon speaker I promise that whispers are going around the room letting everyone know this celebrity lawyer is a CNN regular and when she speaks she has the credibility that comes with fame. People buy her book at the back of the room and jockey for a photo op; all because her PR people got her the CNN gig and she got fame.

While recognition is valuable and credibility is another great benefit, what about money? Fame does not automatically make you rich. There are hundreds of examples of people who achieved immense national fame or even just fame in their community or industry that did not make a dime from their celebrity status.

We're not talking about the Hollywood stars who got the lucky break, thought it would go on forever and squandered their early millions. This is about those people in other fields that captured fame but didn't know how to monetize it.

What we're talking about here is one of the most important messages of the book. Celebrity status is an assured way to get your name in the paper and to be the expert on television but if you don't develop a way to use fame to put food on the table, it's just vanity gone public. So fame can and should also be partially about creating and growing personal wealth.

The money, the recognition and the credibility are all elements of what you get with fame; and remember, anyone who understands the fame formula can have all this. The most fun of it all is that you get to be one of the special people, one of the famous.

You've seen them. They're composed, articulate, and fun. We want to know them; to be like them. The famous are people you would love to have as friends. We want to be near them and we want them to like us. When they arrive anywhere, they unconsciously make an entrance and they don't leave someplace; they make an exit.

What is really cool is that, with work, you can develop these traits and become famous by developing the best authentic you. To discover how it all happens we need to see where it all started: Hollywood, California.

HOLLYWOOD COINS THE PHRASE "MOVIE STARS"

Hollywood executives were the first to spot the cash value of fame and reduce it to a specific film industry fame formula that could be applied to actors, producers, and others in the business. The very first powerful personal brands came from the film industry and every single one was created with the fame formula.

A half century before digital rights, DVDs and product spin offs became the new entertainment industry business model, there were only three money values in the movie business: the films themselves, the actors who became "Stars", and the very visible people who turned these assets into cash – the producers and directors.

With panache, audacity, and an intuitive sense of what the public wanted, the studio executives hardwired magic into the film industry by selecting a handful of genetically beautiful people and giving them real life roles. From Mary Pickford to Rock Hudson and everywhere in between, these people became the idols of the times.

These new celebrities lived a role and the world became a stage around their lives. The Hollywood fame factory didn't just put these new idols into cars; they drove automobiles. Who can deny that any man was simply more attractive when driving a Duesenberg, a Cord, or piloting a classic motor yacht? Similarly, a fantastic looking woman went from small town Potato Festival Queen to top tier celebrity in part by showing a little leg while exiting an Italian convertible.

Studio wardrobe departments, top designers with unlimited budgets, and the very best hair and makeup people, joined voice coaches and acting teachers to polish the studio talent into movie stars. Everyone's role was completely scripted; they knew their parts. And who do you think coined the term Movie Stars? It was people like us – then.

The audacity of the tinsel town fame makers was almost without measure. Take the annual Academy Awards for instance. Although the event's Nielsens have lost their luster, in old Hollywood it was the event of the year. If you analyze Oscar night, it probably started with five studio execs having drinks at some So Cal eatery when someone suggested they actually start giving themselves awards!

What an exceptional idea. Television audiences would eat it up and every studio could trot out their talent with a show that started on the Red Carpet where studio wares, the actors themselves, would be delivered by limousines, each with just the right companion. Publicity people covered pre-parties, arrivals, gowns, couples, countless awards, exits, post parties, the losers and the winners alike.

The result of this publicity coup – being nominated for an award or actually winning one, caused the value of the studios' ultimate product, films, to skyrocket. Every man wanted to be like Rock Hudson and every woman wanted to sleep with him.

Studio photographers captured every moment of the stars' lives but in true film industry style – they would take 150 shots to get "just the right one" which would then be distributed everywhere from the front lines of whatever war was happening at the time to the covers of the magazines that were heavily supported by movie studio advertising and copy.

Hollywood entertained the American public with fame while making immense profits that continue today, all with the fame formula. In reality the Hollywood-created fame influenced the world in much bigger ways. We're convinced that the image of the American Dream created, packaged, distributed, and sold by the film industry enabled the United States to become a

Super Power (a well crafted Washington DC publicity word) as the soldiers of our enemies secreted touched-up pictures of Doris Day at Malibu beach.

Even today Baywatch is insanely popular across all those recently named countries that were part of the old USSR. Who would have thought that Pamela Anderson would do more for world peace than the United Nations?

CELEBRITIES RULE – NEW AMERICAN ROYALTY

While Hollywood used fame to spread the American Dream, it's historically ironic that in doing so they created a class of uniquely American royalty – the Super Elite. The privileged and powerful grew beyond Hollywood to include the successful famous people managing personal roles in several new categories well outside of the entertainment industry.

New celebrities appeared first in the music industry, a logical outgrowth of the film business as music became more about entertainment than art. The fame formula was clearly in play as musicians embraced their elite roles and the public clamored for the most personal details of their lives.

Music industry fame grew from Glen Miller in the 1940s, who grew from band leader to celebrity and finally to legend as he heroically flew into danger's path during the war and didn't make it back. Heroic certainly, but clearly a James Dean or Marilyn Monroe-like example of how much more tragic is the death of our celebs. It's another quirky result of fame; people you never met care when you die.

Concurrent with the growth of music legends like Glen, Elvis, Mick, Madonna and today's crop of music starlets and country hit makers we saw sports royalty arise. Baseball, football and ultimately golf produced a class of the famous that every American boy followed from childhood.

What was so brilliant about Hollywood's marketing of celebrity and stars was that, unlike European royalty which you had to be born into or of the class that could marry into, these celebrities were our neighbors, our schoolmates, our friends who were "discovered" because they were "special" and they made us all believe we could have that too. So, this stardom was not only something we could relate to – but, it was attainable and we all got into it with gusto. In many ways, we continue to do so today.

Somehow an early baseball trading card can easily be worth $50,000 and Tiger Woods can have a billion dollar net worth; this is fame outside of Hollywood. Fame in sports also explains the incredible lives and business branding in the tennis industry; starting with Billie Jean King and Bobby Riggs, Arthur Ashe then on to Jimmy Connors and Chris Evert to the modern day with the Williams sisters and whatever 17 year old superstar is thrilling the cameras today – on and off the court.

As the world became ever more fame-obsessed and every sector demanded more leaders in the spotlight, the next logical celebrities came into play. In our country, which is based on money, business titans grew from the modest early legends of Vanderbilt, Crocker, Henry Ford to modern-day tech gods Jobs, Gates and the rest of the Forbes 400.

Malcolm Forbes and his Forbes Magazine grasped early the public's desire to connect with the famous. While Hollywood and gossip magazines were chronicling the daily lives of the entertainment stars, Forbes Magazine was doing the same in the business sector. Stars were born, brands like Donald Trump became possible and there became a very direct presentation of that sexiest of all combinations: fame and money.

The same formula is followed by Fast Company Magazine and others as the idea of business fame expands like the universe with new galaxies of stars being created. It was quite a trip from Cornelius Vanderbilt to whatever global technology kid is the latest billionaire; but that trip was powered by fame as business people joined the super elite.

So, do you have to land a big movie role, whip Serena at Wimbledon, or invent the next killer software app to become part of the new royal class? No, and that's the whole point of Fame 101. Fame is the ticket to becoming one of the super elite and anyone, in any field can gain admission. There are neither boundaries nor any limitations on the number of people invited to step behind life's velvet ropes.

All you need is fame to play and it's available to those people who have the formula, then use it to create an interesting unique role for themselves that captures and maintains the attention of a community. Celebrities in every field do indeed rule – they're the new American royalty.

YOUR MAXIMUM AUTHENTIC SELF

Fame is special and few will do what it takes to earn it for themselves. It would however be much easier to grasp if there were a simple definition, but likely at this point in your reading you understand it's a force of life, different for every person, rather than something that can be defined.

We've already uncovered some things about fame that you probably knew intuitively from observing real life, but perhaps never realized it was something you could use for your own success. Consider these several points as you move forward through Fame 101:

- Fame is way beyond money, although it can deliver wealth as one of its benefits. It's a powerful tool you can use to get many things that money can't buy.
- Fame is based to some extent on showmanship. The successful fame seekers use entertainment industry concepts and techniques to promote themselves.
- Fame is the key to admission into the special group we call

society's super elite. You're not invited to join this community; when you create a place for yourself you simply become part of it.

- Fame determines who succeeds and who doesn't in many cases. It's an unbeatable competitive edge in any industry or life sector.

Ideally you see that fame gives you hidden advantages in everything you do; it magnifies your actions and it maximizes your results. The remainder of Fame 101 looks at the many things you can do to build a powerful personal brand around yourself to become the best authentic you – only famous.

If you have *any* doubt that fame can be yours, consider that Mary Kate & Ashley Olsen are a billion dollar industry, that one of the country's best known lawyers was at the bottom of his class at a third-tier law school, and that the author keynoting at your industry convention simply used the formula you'll learn from Fame 101 to cause people to elevate them onto the stage.

Fame, as we write about and create, is very specifically creating your Maximum Authentic Self. The finished product is really you, but it's the you that is hidden just beneath your present self. Your famous self is a media trained, polished, informed, and prepared genuine you.

Fame is simply a better and more effective way to live your life. Now let's look at how you can harness its power to catapult yourself to the peak of your profession in about a year.

WHO'S GOT FAME?

THE ELITE AND HOW THEY GOT THERE

. . . .

"We are drawn to someone who 'makes it' in any field which in turn makes them an even bigger celebrity. Professional fame is much more about momentum and personal branding than hype."

—Maggie Jessup

. . . .

KENNEDY FAMILY FAME MACHINE

Old Joe Kennedy was a character and very, very smart. He made crazy amounts of money in the first half of the 1900s, had a huge family, and believed that they should rule the world, or at least the most powerful nation. Joe Kennedy might very well have been the first non-Hollywood person to discover and use the power of fame; unless you go way back to Julius Caesar, Alexander the Great and some others but in modern times let's say it was Ambassador Kennedy; JFK's father.

Joe founded and funded the fanfare that became the Kennedy Family Fame Machine. We learned a lot from studying America's first fame family. Their fame rollout took place over decades and demonstrated every element of the fame formula orchestrated with inspiring artistry. We're certain that the day each male child was born, Joe had their fame plan defined.

The Kennedy legacy started with compelling images. Most of us have boxes of old yellowing photos, news clips, graduation announcements, and low-quality video chronicling our family history. Have you ever wondered how the Kennedy family has so many ideal photo images and such great videos?

Joe Kennedy had professional photographers and some of the earliest videographers capturing his family's every prepared moment. Family football action photos taken on the estate's lawn showed how healthy and happy they all were, but how is it they were often wearing white with no grass stains in the midst of lawn football?

What's more, any photographer will confirm that it's difficult to get a perfect profile shot of a single person in a small boat with not one ripple in the water and yet every Kennedy has a thoughtful inspiring pose captured in just such a spot.

Eldest son, Young Joe, was set to become President of the United States, but was killed in World War II so John Fitzgerald Kennedy, the next son, stepped up. As he won his first political seat there is no doubt Old Joe had funded the wisest of political advisors, publicity pros, and the earliest of image consultants. Most important, these advisors were kept on *after* each election to maximize the brand until the next election.

The Kennedys were the first to utilize television in order to connect with the masses. You know the rest; this magical Son of America made it to the White House with seemingly effortless charm and as a media-magnet. His brief time as President of the United States was even branded: Camelot.

The perfect wife Jackie, who became a huge brand in her own right, wowed the world, undoubtedly with street teams preceding her to countries on her international visits. Note this is the very same formula used by Elvis and the Beatles to assure flag waving crowds at every stop.

Did you ever wonder how hundreds of people in those crowds "just happened to have" all the same size flags, as well as bouquets and roses to throw? Was John John's perfect salute at his father's funeral suggested by media-wise Jackie or another advisor? Was that not one of the most compelling images of a generation?

Fast forward to now and the Kennedy family has had the worst of tragedies as well as the most glorious of triumphs. The deaths of Bobby, John John, and others were all the more epic because of their fame. The family fame continues because they all realize the value of continuous brand promotion. Any Kennedy son, daughter, distant cousin or spouse is a "Get" for a party or fundraiser, admission to the elite university of their choice is automatic, and they have a huge edge when vying for elected offices or jobs.

We could write a volume on Kennedy family brand strategy but the question arises: Do we think they're bad people for promoting themselves into positions of power? Absolutely not. Perhaps just the opposite.

This family has used their well-crafted fame platform to do some remarkable things for our country and they continue to do great works.

Our point is that they are an ideal multi-generational illustration of how to use fame to have high-impact as well as to have the broadest audience for your message and mission. Some of the fame perks of wealth, popularity and access are the byproducts of fame and the Kennedy family has worked hard to achieve them.

POLITICS

While John, Bobby and Ted Kennedy were growing up on an idyllic East Coast estate, a young actor by the name of Ronald Reagan was learning the Art of Fame in Hollywood. Who would have thought this B movie regular, co-staring with an ape in one film, would become one of our country's most charismatic leaders and ultimately set into motion the events which would end the Cold War?

President Reagan, together with fame-wise wife Nancy, brought Hollywood Glamour to politics. As a follow up to his acting career, with communication skills honed on movie sets and with a bevy of film-industry supporters, Reagan set his sights on the California governor's mansion.

This was a smart first step because Californians of the time were more open to new things than citizens of any other state and the idea of an actor running the world's 8th largest economy wasn't any crazier than other things going on at the time from Berkeley to Beverly Hills.

Reagan had charisma and knew how to market it. Hollywood's strongest legacy stars got behind him, as did every woman who ever heard him speak. Governor Reagan played to the cameras, had rock solid scripted messaging, "performed" with style and his fame team fanned the flames of his brand around the country.

Ultimately Ronald Reagan became President Reagan and skipped the pitfall that crashes so many new-famers; he knew his limitations and surrounded himself with some of the smartest people in the country. Reagan affirmed what Kennedy had launched; a mediagenic candidate with a continuously stoked fame platform became the new formula for a winning politician.

Governor Pro-Wrestler and Governor Terminator, who coincidentally is married to a Kennedy spin-off brand, followed with great success. Both crushed their opponents with style, drama, publicity, and strong platforms. President Clinton sold Hollywood style charisma to finesse out of business scandals, intern embarrassments, and away from a gaggle of fame-seeking former bed partners.

Wasn't he impeached? And yet somehow he continued in office because he was so darned visible, likeable, and the media loved him. This is the essence and result of fame.

Although Bush Jr. tried to capture the fame formula with carrier landings, a Mission Accomplished sign, and by taking out evil dictators, his administration marked a go-back to back room politics rather than charismatic leadership.

And then came Obama. Following the fame drought of the Bush presidency, the country was ready for a dramatic change. Who more unlikely a candidate than an inexperienced young African American from a state with a history of political machining? On the other hand, who more likely than a New Media savvy player with Hollywood looks, style and messaging.

John McCain didn't know what hit him. Although Senator McCain make a heroic fame play with Sarah Palin's candidacy, that excitement peaked early and was over when Katie Couric, a fame pro in her own right, put a stake through the heart of Sarah's early popularity.

The Obama machine declared an almost unanimous victory, far from the truth, but that didn't matter to America; the people were ready for President Obama – the ultimate brand. Many weak state and local candidates were even swept into office countrywide because they were Democrats. At the time if you weren't pro-Obama, you were un-American; at least so said the majority of the media, the ultimate arbiters of who gets fame and who will keep it.

NOTHING'S SACRED – MOTHER TERESA'S PUBLICITY TEAM

Most people believe that celebrity personal branding, or fame, went national when television became something more than a novelty right about the time of the Kennedy – Nixon debates. One was mediagenic, one wasn't – guess who won? However, our country's elders remember the Glory Days of Radio.

Families would sit around the radio on Sunday nights and radio was how several national personal brands were rolled out. It was the medium where the country got its news; we still hear Franklin Delano Roosevelt's voice telling the world that the Pearl Harbor attack was "A day that will live in infamy."

Well, just after World War II in 1950 an unknown evangelist by the name of Billy Graham launched a radio show in Portland, Oregon. Reverend Graham almost intuitively understood celebrity and fame with all its elements and used it to grow one small radio show into a $200 million worldwide ministry. Early on he defined a niche for himself as someone different from the tent-show white-suited traveling fiery evangelists of the time.

His niche was based on integrity and rock-solid consistent messaging. While some may not agree with his message you would be hard put to find someone who would doubt his sincerity and uprightness. We'll skip past the products and fundraising efforts that are part of all commercial ministries today as we saw the Reverend Billy Graham become spiritual advisor to president after president.

He has Secret Service protection and is regarded as a national treasure. What a terrific way to demonstrate the use of fame to impact the world. Fame isn't all about Britney Spears going nuts, Lindsay Lohan showing off, or other Hollywood bad girls; fame can give you the platform from which you can affect a million or a hundred million people.

Jump ahead until the late 90's and witness the launch of three major faith based brands: Joel Osteen, Max Lucado and Rick Warren. Each used a combination of fame elements to build huge ministries and to create for themselves a wide footprint on the faith landscape.

You can see Joel Osteen speaking at his Lakewood Church on television several nights a week. His television ministry did so well he purchased the Compaq Center in Houston for his "church". A phenomenal showman with a feel good message, Joel packs in a crowd of 18,000 faith filled followers each and every week. His book *Your Best Life Now* hit the best seller list in its first week; his income is well into the millions annually and it's clear he used fame to leap to the top of the crowded television ministry group.

Just behind Joel is a quiet Church of Christ pastor from San Antonio, Texas – Max Lucado. The Church of Christ is surely one of the more conservative denominations eschewing even musical instruments in their services. And yet, Max has positively leapt from the pulpit to achieve national prominence; he's even a Larry King regular.

He speaks with a quiet sure voice to crowds of thousands, his church grounds are a compound of impressive scale, and there are Max Lucado books and DVDs selling millions of copies throughout the world.

Somehow amidst all this fame, Max has maintained a quiet non-Osteen like demeanor consistent with his beliefs. He doesn't need to put on a show because his platform and message are so solidly built. He demonstrates that sometimes it's easier to capture a crowd with a quiet voice whether on Larry King or at the Portland Rose Garden.

Rick Warren, a pastor from San Diego, California used technology to build the largest Baptist congregation in the nation – 75,000 at last count. His book *A Purpose Driven Life* has sold a million copies with spin off books and products rolling out at a prodigious rate. He built a National brand from a local congregation.

If there was any doubt that Rick had hit the top of his field, his invitation to do the invocation at the Obama inauguration removed that doubt. As President Obama began his administration trying to heal a country divided after the longest election season in history, Rick Warren was the token gift to the Bush faith-based conservatives among whom it was hard to find an Obama supporter.

Finally, the title of this subchapter is Mother Theresa's Publicity Team. She was an exceptionally fine person and was ultimately sainted by the Catholic Church. But, what differentiated her and her model of service from the thousands of other nuns out there working amidst the world's most wretched?

Not to diminish her incredible work in even the slightest, but she accomplished more because she became an international brand. Suffice it to say that the Vatican has a publicity team worthy of any Hollywood studio and they have understood the value of fame for many centuries. When focused on the diminutive Mother Theresa of Calcutta, she became one of the most powerful personal brands in history and ultimately a saint. Yet another example of using fame for the forces of good and God.

THE HELP BECOME CELEBRITIES

None of our observations in the political or religious fame fields likely surprised you but there is a new generation of celebrities in completely counterintuitive categories who certainly surprised us when they launched.

Suddenly in this upside down world cooks, construction workers, and beauticians are the new social royalty as a result of solid personal branding, exceptional publicity, and creative use of the media: all fame elements.

When we were kids the cooks had to use the kitchen entrance, construction workers were expected to stay pretty much outside, and the beauty parlor was the only career option for girls who didn't make it to college. No more; for those with fame it's now red carpets and Lamborghinis.

Let's have a look at the cooks first. James Beard and Julia Child followed closely by Wolfgang Puck were among the most successful nationally branded chefs and were responsible for differentiating the "cooks" from the "chefs" and preparing the world to accept the concept of the celebrity chef.

This isn't to say there weren't well-known chefs in most cities but James, Julia, and Wolfgang played the media, charmed their restaurant patrons, rolled out collateral products like cookbooks and endorsed frozen dinners as early masters of riding the fame machine to national prominence.

Following their pioneering brand efforts came a fascinating mix of successful celebs, developing niches for themselves in this new field. Now we have a Chicago mom, a slightly abrasive Northeasterner, and a Southern icon blazing the fame trail in the food vertical.

Emeril has a television show with branded products while Rachael Ray climbed from in-store pitchgirl to Nielsen-darling and magazine magnate in a startlingly short period. And what about Paula Dean? She's cobbler'd her way to the peak of New South society with a restaurant you can't get into, a Savannah waterfront mansion, and some reality television and movie roles on the side.

Even Paula's brother picked up enough spin off celebrity to open the exceptional restaurant Bubba's. We should note that fame gives the access to capital and customers to open a restaurant but at the end of the day the food is what will bring people back.

In the world of celebrity it's now even hip to be a construction worker, although as in every other fame category you must be in the top one percent in terms of visibility or you're just another person in a plastic hat pounding in nails. The category opened up with the This Old House television show where elitist homeowners learned to restore their declining homesteads.

The next phase was Bob Vila, the first celebrity construction worker and now there are teams of "designers" with sledge hammers and tool belts who come to unsuspecting couples' homes, insult their décor and proceed to take out walls, cabinets, kitchens and landscaping. New shrubs, some chrome kitchen appliances and elegant faux wood accents, and Bam! (to quote Emeril), there's a tasteful home – all quarterbacked by a supermodel in a hardhat.

Moving on to hair gurus; who can name a famous barber or beauty parlor operator from before the 1970s? Vidal Sassoon helped the country make the leap from barbers and beauty parlors to stylists and salons with all of the fame elements supported by smart marketing.

Great graphics and ten foot photos of fantastically tressed models was the stage he created and together with his wife Beverly, he played the Vidal Sassoon role masterfully. The result? A complete change in perception of the American and then the world public. Franchising and a hot product line were close behind.

John Paul Mitchell played the role of homeless guy turned hair product guru with panache: American Dream realized with a great fame platform. He followed close in Vidal's footsteps but a broader field was launched with Jose Eber who became a Hair Celebrity.

Any time Entertainment Tonight or even some reality show even touch the subject of hair, there he is with scissors putting on a show of, well simply cutting hair but he does put on a great show, chats up the host and audiences love him. Following in his footsteps is a gaggle of would-be famous stylists measuring their worth by who they "do".

So what can we learn about fame from superstylists, celebrity chefs, and hot looking contractors? We learn that anything is possible and anyone, yes anyone can have fame. There are no limits and don't be surprised when an airport shoe shine guy is thanking us all in a few years during his Emmy acceptance speech.

MEDICAL STARS –
DOCTORS WHO PLAY ONE ON TV AND RADIO

Every field has its celebrities and none shine brighter than Celebrity Doctors, both medical doctors and PhDs. About a dozen docs have captured the minds, eyes and wallets of America by offering us weight loss or youth, addressing our neuroses, or selling us karmic peace. All of these aside, there is one MD who has built a brand around being a qualified great guy who reports to us the latest in health news.

Dr. Sanjay Gupta is a compelling example of what can be done with a bit of charisma, an MD, and some great personal brand building. Sanjay was an advisor to power-brand Senator Hillary Clinton and CNN invented the term Chief Medical Correspondent to give viewers a method to accept this cool new brand.

While Dr. Gupta has a few detractors, he has taken on the mantle of America's doctor previously filled to lesser degrees by Dr. Bob Arnott, C. Everett Koop and a few others. Has he hit superstardom? Consider his column in Time Magazine, his bestselling book Chasing Life, or his coveted spot on People Magazine's World's Sexiest Men list. His great branding and fame have reportedly placed him on the short list for Surgeon General in the Obama administration.

There are many people who have leveraged their MD's in creative ways. Consider the following doctors: Authors Robin Cook, Michael Crichton and Sir Arthur Conan Doyle, Self help guru Deepak Chopra, POTUS aspirants Howard Dean, Ron Paul and Bill Frist, Revolutionary Ché Guevara, and even Maria Montessori and Pope John XXI.

As medical doctors hold a special status in society, there is little doubt these notables were able to use the MD credibility to capture opportunities otherwise unavailable. The American public is absolutely captivated by doctors; consider the television show Grey's Anatomy where fantastic looking people are made even sexier by an MD suffix. House and others follow suit with Nip 'n Tuck and reality plastic surgery shows topping the ratings. Dr. Perricone is the latest diet book MD with a seven figure author income prior to even showing up at the medical office.

Let us not forget Dr. Oz who, after being launched on Oprah, has become a household name. He has produced several best sellers and has his own television show following Dr. Phil's lead (another Oprah-endorsed brand). His daughter even has a book out, *The Dorm Room Diet.*

PhDs are nearly as easily celebrity brandable because of the Dr. prefix. At least 60% of American radio listeners don't know or care about the MD – PhD distinction and millions look to Dr. Laura for advice. She has sold millions of books to people with turbulent personal lives and gives sound byte advice daily on stations around the world.

Sometimes an image can capture a brand and for us this happened with Dr. Laura. This last year we saw one of those rock star fifty foot limos with two motorcycle escorts parked in the no-loading zone in front of Wal Mart.

The celebrity? Inside the store was Dr. Laura, surrounded by security and a line of fans waiting up to an hour to get her signature in a book. Phenomenal personal branding and spectacular use of an advanced degree in physiology. Her success? It's clearly not her looks; it is absolutely her fame platform.

What about the top cancer or heart docs? There are stars in these and other serious medical fields but they are microcelebrities within their niches; very few have broken out to become medical rock stars although quite a few have tried with some well written but commercially unsuccessful books.

The world loves doctors and it doesn't matter whether they're MDs, PhDs or simply play one on TV. But, we'll only give them fame if they tell us how to lose weight, perk up our boobs or tell us how to deal with our straying spouse or ungrateful child.

NOT JUST ANOTHER PRETTY FACE –
BRILLIANTLY BRANDED BABES

When Cheryl Tiegs coined the term Supermodel she thought she was simply trying out some fresh personal branding to boost her own career. The reality is that Cheryl, the first Supermodel, opened a whole new category of celebrity that took models from the catwalk to the boardroom.

Prior to Cheryl Tiegs models were seen only as runway and fashion-photo figures, most indistinguishable from the rest – really beautiful and insanely thin. A few standouts including Bianca Jagger and Twiggy from the 60's amped up the profession by becoming the first highly paid models – they were earning six figures per year. Until Ms. Tiegs that was the pinnacle of the profession.

Christie Brinkley joined Cheryl as their careers grew from highly paid fashion models into endorsement deals for cosmetics and clothing lines; they were stars in their own right so they were able to transfer that halo effect to products to enhance desirability and price. These Supermodels hit the seven figure earnings mark quickly, redefining their profession.

You would think that a few million a year for a pretty face would be about as far as Supermodeldom could go but then along came Cindy Crawford. Cindy is beautiful but not necessarily more so than a thousand or two other models you can see daily in Los Angeles, New York, Paris or Milan. But, Cindy was brilliant as relates to using the fame machine.

She had a team of publicity people, image consultants, marketing gurus, agents and financial dealmakers constantly promoting and monetizing her brand. She was able to stay in play for many years beyond the typical five year maximum with multiple major endorsement deals and then movie roles as befit this latest generation of Supermodel. Cindy crept into the low eight figures for earnings.

The saga continued in the post-Cindy era with Heidi Klum and Claudia Schiffer. They applied the formula implemented by Cindy but started earlier in their career and thus were able to get farther. They made the leap from endorsements to having their own merchandise and jumped well into the eight figure earning range. Heidi Klum made the Forbes Magazine Celebrity 100 for earnings, joining the likes of Oprah Winfrey and Tiger Woods on this elite list.

Believe it or not, the saga continues with the super popular Reality TV show, hosted by the former Supermodel Tyra Banks: America's Next Top Model. Successful television shows make amazing amounts of money. You might remember that Wheel of Fortune catapulted Merv Griffin to billionaire status. So Tyra's on that path.

What's next for this fame category? Just when we think these brilliantly branded babes have peaked, we forecast a Supermodel running for office; perhaps even entering the California governor's race. Couldn't happen? Might we remind you that Conan the Barbarian is currently enjoying his second term in office? Anything's possible with fame.

MILLIONAIRE MECHANICS AND CEL-"AB"-RITIES

There's an aura of fun and cool around hot cars in America so it's understandable there would be a celebrity contingent in the racing arena. When automobiles were in their infancy, America and the world followed the antics of daredevil racers with Phil Hill being the first big brand.

As time passed there were very few new notables until Mario Andretti came along and the Formula One driver became something more than a simple driver. High end racing is all about endorsements and Andretti knew how to play the fame game to his advantage. Racing wins, beautiful women, international settings and very fast cars; he became a household name – constantly promoted by publicity pros.

More recent automotive legends grew out of America's heartland: the NASCAR drivers. The early ones were actually what put NASCAR on the road to becoming what it is now America's most popular sport. Dale Earnhardt and Richard Petty brought media attention and ultimately ticket sales to the serious profitability level by developing their own fame platforms.

NASCAR itself made its next big leap using the fame formula: charismatic drivers with Hollywood looks, dressed for the part. Dale Earnhardt Jr. follows in his famous father's footsteps with seven figure endorsements. Dale and another dozen auto celebs look like they should be on the latest One Tree Hill episode and risk their lives weekly on national television; the ultimate human drama at more than 200 miles per hour.

It's easy to understand the fame following the NASCAR drivers gather but what about the mechanics? As amazing as it may sound, but conclusively proving our theory that fame can be created in any field, some mechanics and auto body guys have created a fame niche for themselves.

Tom and Ray, the NPR radio mechanics, share auto repair tips on 588 stations from Brooklyn to Guam. Somehow middle aged northeasterners have joined the rich and famous by deftly handling call-ins from Volvo owners looking for a quick clutch fix. Is their success a fluke? A one time capture of the bottom end of the auto fame niche? No, it's the fame formula and they're not alone in their four wheeled celebrity.

Popular television shows including American Chopper, Pimp My Ride and some clones have captured America's television watching hearts by showing us how to add horsepower, install flatscreens into our headrests, and find the best paint solution for our classic pickups. MTV, known as the creators of cool for a generation, continues with season after season of these new celebrities turning old horrible cars into collectors items and the body guys into superstars.

Change the channel away from an immaculate mechanic demonstrating the installation of a differential in a monster truck and you might well see one of the Cel-"Ab"-rities. An infomercial industry has sprung up around selling us an easy route to having a flat stomach. Apparently America has an overwhelming desire for six-pack abdominal muscles and we'll back it up with cash – lots of it.

Fame and celebrity sells almost anything while the potential profits are enormous in off-hour television selling. To understand where this comes from, note that infomercials, sometimes known as home shopping, are a billion dollar industry. It's no surprise then that B-list television star Chuck Norris, the aging but impressive retired supermodel Christie Brinkley, and career ditz-player Suzanne Sommers have made a mint selling us machinery that will flatten our abs, strengthen our thighs and take ten years off our bottoms.

Just as celebrities created the ab-improvement industry, exercise gurus have made themselves famous with quick fitness fixes. Billy Blanks is famous for just one thing, Tae Bo but it has indeed given him fame. He can always get a table at a top Hollywood eatery and it's all from out-exercising his predecessor on the fame highway, Richard Simmons, who might be the only non-ballet male to have become famous while wearing a leotard. He too can get a table anywhere.

EVERYDAY MICRO CELEBRITIES

You can see the theme here as we look at Who's Got Fame from the greats to the silly. It's all about fame; it can be found or created everywhere. It's the same formula whether you're a Kennedy child or a New York cabbie with your own reality show. Fame isn't always in the highly visible arenas of politics or television.

There are micro celebrities in every field and they're the ones who "get" this fame thing and use it to place themselves above the clutter in every industry. Have you ever had a Mrs. Fields cookie at the mall? Is this just a name? No, it was fame-smart Debbie Fields who took a cookie recipe and with some great publicists and brand strategy folks made some serious dough from her international celebrity.

Do you know the name Meg Whitman? If you're around the technology industry you know her as Ebay's chief executive officer. She is clearly a micro celebrity who is on everyone's A list. What is her background and what caused her meteoric rise to the top in a very competitive field?

Prior to Ebay Meg was the one who brought back the Mr. Potatohead brand. She scored a leading role for the tired spud-toy in the movie Toy Story. She picked up some serious visibility with the film industry ties and now she's at the top of the tech world. Is she done? Can she go farther with her celebrity? You already know the answer, of course because there are no limits to this fun fame thing. She has formed an exploratory group to run for Governor of California. Why not? The ex-Terminator is finishing his second term.

We all know other examples of micro-celebrities from television and the entertainment shows that some people call the news. Remember the gaggle of legal talent around OJ Simpson during his media circus? Ten lawyers were sometimes physically shoving each other out of the way to get television time.

All of those lawyers played their participation in the trial into very lucrative careers with four of them making the leap to superstardom. The late Johnny Cochran hit superstardom with his dramatic line "If it doesn't fit you must acquit" and Alan Dershowitz made it from Harvard law professor to CNN sometimes-correspondent.

Who learned about the beauty of micro-celebrity in the OJ legal proceedings? Not Cato Calin although he picked up some television time, nor Judge Ito who became almost the caricature of the media-grabbing judge. The big dollar instant-famers were Marcia Clark and Christopher Darden.

Marcia started the trial as an earnest prosecutor going after the bad guy with no clue about fame but mid-trial she went from budget wardrobe and home perm to Armani with a designer hairstyle. Her publicist was issuing statements; suddenly she was "represented" by an agent and she picked up a seven figure book deal following a spectacular Loss. The public didn't care if she won or lost. She was a celebrity and everyone wanted to know her.

Playing second chair to Marcia was the quiet Christopher Darden who, although he didn't embrace the celebrity as did Marcia, garnered a television role and a fat book deal; all from being the assistant to a prosecuting attorney who lost a criminal trial. Fame can sprout up anywhere and Marcia Clark and Christopher Darden became overnight millionaires by understanding fame.

WHO'S NEXT?

From Paula Deen to President Obama these are just a few of the people who have fame and are using it to maximize their footprint on the world. Another hundred examples of the creation and use of fame are scattered throughout the book but from this chapter we hope you learned about fame by example.

FAME 101

THE FAME FORMULA

CREATING THE
SUPER ELITE

· ·

"We discovered how to put someone in the spotlight and keep them there; we call our methodology the fame formula. It's a blueprint anyone can use to capture and monetize this powerful force."

—Maggie Jessup

· ·

HERE IT IS – THE FORMULA THAT CREATES THE SUPER ELITE OF EVERY FIELD

If you're impatient and jumped to the very foundation of Fame 101 so you could have the formula for fame, we'll make it easy for you:

Fame = Personal Branding + Publicity + Brand You Marketing + Personal Financial Development + Brand Longevity Strategies.

It's really that simple, not to be confused with easy, and it can work for anyone. This formula, which we've taken a decade to develop and understand, is the proven process for making it to the top of your field, reaping the benefits, and keeping that elite position for life.

Using the fame formula a priest became a pope, an unknown local television weather girl became Oprah, a caterer working out of her house became Brand Martha, a homeless writer became best selling author J.D. Rowling, and it's exactly how the successful Leading Voice of your own industry captured that lofty position.

Our business is making people famous and that's where the fame formula came from. We studied the successful brands from Alexander the Great to Benjamin Franklin to Billy Graham and ultimately to brand Obama. Although these people and the 100 others we studied could not possibly be more diverse in their activities, they all rose to the top with an intuitive or learned understanding of the activities that create fame.

What is truly amazing is we found that anyone can catapult themselves to the top of their field in about a year, definitely in less than two, with the correct mix of the fame elements: personal brand strategy, personal marketing, publicity and personal evolution. There are no shortcuts; we've looked for them and watched people fall off a fame trajectory by trying to skip a step. So don't look for a way to skip past any part of the fame formula; it won't work.

Applying the fame formula is hard work and most people don't have the resolution to do what it takes to make it happen for themselves; millions think about it, tens of thousands take a run at it, thousands make it pretty far along, but only a few hundred of any generation join society's elite. It's these people we call famous. They're the ones who did the work and stuck to it long enough to achieve that fame.

People want to know them, meet them, elect them to office, give them the best tables, make sure they get front row tickets, and make sure they are financially successful beyond the dreams of the common man. Fame is nothing less than using what's unique about yourself to become a powerful personal brand; it's fun, it's cool, it is excitement beyond measure – it's fame and you can have it.

The formula is in your hands: your first step is reading the rest of the book – remember there are neither shortcuts nor free rides although you can do all this with little or no money. This chapter gives you a 30,000 foot level look at each element of the formula so you can have a sense of how it all works together as you study the details throughout the book.

PUBLICITY – THE TICKET TO VERY BIG VISIBILITY

Our formula is the recipe for fame and publicity, the first element, is the yeast or catalyst in that recipe; it's what makes everything else work to its maximum effect. Whether you are an entertainer, Chief Executive Officer, or a garden guy, you will not achieve the peak of your profession without it. The top people in your field know the power of publicity and they use it to their advantage.

Publicity is how:

- CISCO's CEO John Chambers is selected to be on the cover of Fast Company magazine so frequently.

- Christina Applegate heads this last year's People Magazine 100 Most Beautiful People list and how most of the others made the list too.
- Some people get $5,000 to $25,000 for a forty minute speaking engagement while others in their field are fighting to speak for free at the local Kiwanis Club.
- Ninety nine percent of the famous capture the media's spotlight and keep it.

And publicity is how authors get on talk shows, candidates get media coverage, actors build recognition, and it's that special ingredient in the fame process that enables a professional in any field to leap from the pack to become a powerful personal brand.

Being in the media keeps you visible and creates an implied endorsement of your personal brand that our society, correctly or incorrectly, accepts as more valuable. Publicity gets you that media. A physician, florist or charity head jumps ahead of the competition with one People Magazine profile. An Oprah appearance can put your brand into the stratosphere.

Publicity confounds the accountants; it is absolutely impossible to quantify and yet it typically offers the best return on investment when used properly. If you have any doubt ask yourself whether you would give more credibility to a plastic surgeon who has full-page color ads in Scottsdale Magazine every month for six months or to a provider who had a weekly column in the Phoenix newspaper or a profile of her in its Sunday supplement.

Unfortunately for many, publicity is likely the most misunderstood fame element. People confuse advertising with publicity and they think publicity is all about getting your name in the paper. Publicity is critical to your success and you must understand some basic definitions in order to fully absorb the fame formula.

Publicity is based on the situation that every day, sometimes twice a day, newspapers must fill thousands of column inches with something; the same with magazines although most of those are monthly – still lots of column inches. Television news shows, evening magazines, as well as radio must create hours of programming every single day; even when there isn't anything super newsworthy going on.

To capture some of those column inches or minutes of television time, your publicist connects with the right person who decides what goes on and what doesn't. They pitch that person with the idea and ideally the client gets coverage. Publicists are the people who create and manage publicity. Publicity in turn starts when a publicist connects with a journalist to present an idea for a story, typically featuring or including one of the publicist's clients.

There are many ways for the publicist to make the connection but the first connection is customarily pitching the idea on a phone call or email Note here that the "pitch" is not a press release; many people stumble here because they skip this vital direct connection effort. Many believe a press release is sufficient to draw the media to their door but this is old school thinking.

The press release, which years ago was an effective first communication tool, has become almost valueless due to overuse or at least when distributed randomly with no phone or email connection prior to that distribution. So, a pitch is a short and instantly intriguing communication between the publicist and a member of the media.

As an example of an effective pitch, consider the lead might be: Most People Don't Know that Kiefer Sutherland has a Twin or Have you heard that a doctor in Los Angeles has isolated the gene that makes people obese? And he's got an inexpensive method to turn it off. Whatever your field, and it doesn't have to be as high profile as entertainment or medicine, strategically used publicity will get you in the media.

This is publicity in a nutshell; we'll talk more about each of these steps and how to use publicity to enhance your personal brand throughout this book, but for now let's have a look at the next fame element – creating a powerful personal brand.

PERSONAL BRANDING - CREATING POWER BRAND "YOU"

The very basis of fame is having a Powerful Personal Brand; becoming the NIKE of your field. Anyone can name a dozen or more huge personal brands like Oprah, Tiger, Heidi, Donald, or Martha; no one can doubt their power. Each of these brands creates a definite emotional response when we hear it spoken and a multi-billion dollar industry has grown up around turning personal brands like these into money. Our next section will be on monetizing your personal brand but for now let's look at exactly what personal branding is all about.

We live in a branded world; it's impossible to buy a golf shirt without a logo; FedEx, UPS, AOL, ABC, CNN and other acronym-companies spend fortunes on branding and their efforts cover much more than logos; it's the whole brand experience. A foundational element of the fame formula requires you to accept that you, yourself are a brand, just like Coca Cola or Target Stores.

The next step is learning lessons from these big brands; it's one secret to standing out from the crowd and prospering, whatever your field. You're in charge of Brand You and creating, building and marketing it should be the defining force of all your professional efforts. This applies to candidates, actors, authors, real estate professionals, doctors, attorneys... anyone.

If you're working in a corporate structure, branding can make you a valuable free agent – you're lending your brand to whatever company is paying you at that time but you have big value on the open market; at least if you build yourself into a powerful personal brand.

Great personal branding is the difference between being the vice president of product development at a company and being that "Hot New Creative Guy we've got on a two-year contract." Same position, same person – quadruple the perceived value and likely quadruple the compensation. The fame formula focuses on building you into one of these powerful brands.

Once you accept that branding principles apply to you, the first pro-active effort is to create a unique role for yourself. This is a value that you very visibly bring to the market and a set of feelings or emotions that the mention of your brand creates among your target market.

There is a lot of material on creating your role, your value and your brand in Fame 101, but remember at its core the effort is to create the best authentic you; not something superficial or something that doesn't ring true. The market intuitively spots phonies and bars them from fame; the same market heavily rewards uniqueness and above all, authenticity. This of course doesn't mean being too casual, untrained or unprepared; what we're talking about is your Best authentic self.

Personal branding starts with taking the time to define your role out in the world; what is that thing that makes you special, makes you remarkable, and makes you different? If you can describe that difference in 20 words or less, and it's the best authentic you, you have completed the most important step in personal branding.

Unfortunately, most people haven't taken the time to take on this exercise and thus they're still that vice president of product development at a big brand corporation rather than the micro-celebrity product development guru we described above. And, for those people who have taken the time to design their 20 word personal brand description: is it effective? Is it concise? Does it convey power?

A test of your short description of your brand is to ask yourself whether or not someone would do a double take at a dinner party when you delivered that message. Would your statement suddenly grab their interest? Would they be eager to hear more? This is especially true when working in your target market but it should be sufficiently interesting to capture an outsider's interest as well because a positive result there is indicative of how your brand will be received by the mainstream media; a necessary partner in building a powerful brand.

So, what's your pitch? How do you present your brand? If you don't know, get to work on this foundational element of your success. Time spent in this area can yield lifelong rewards. The how-to part of creating your personal elevator pitch, your 20 word personal brand description, is found in its own section later in the book. Now that we've looked at your role, the next brand step is defining the playing field.

EXPAND YOUR BRAND PLAYING FIELD

The fame formula requires you to develop a powerful personal brand; you know this and you now see how to identify Brand You. The next step in your personal branding process will follow the path of Pepsi, Amazon and the other big company brands. This requires you to identify the industry or arena you're playing in and we encourage you to think broadly here because it's the breadth of your playing field that will be the only limit on your personal success.

What we mean by broadly is best understood by example: you're not an international patent attorney specializing in solidifying the rights of your clients in Southeastern Asian countries; rather, you're an intellectual property lawyer. This is the broader arena where you work and this broadening allows you to develop and capture more opportunities.

If the media needs a talking head on any intellectual property matter, you're eligible. If a sportswear company needs a law firm to take over all their international patent work, you're eligible. This is often a hard concept to grasp as, especially after a decade of working in a field to become a micro specialist, you're asked to comment on something outside of your expertise – there's a hesitancy and that can be a fame killer. Just assume if you're a patent lawyer you can comment for a few minutes on any related subject, given some time to prepare. We'll talk a lot more about this later.

For another personal brand expansion example, you're not the manager of a mid-size company that sells custom blogging software to medical and legal professionals; rather, you're a social media guru. You can see where we're going here; for branding purposes you must create some room for yourself and your brand to grow. So whatever you're doing, whether actor or candidate or florist – expand your definition of your brand out one or two levels to create a geometrically larger market.

Here's a test on the concept. One candidate for mayor in Seattle, Washington is focused on the issue of building a light rail system to connect this spread-out metropolis. What's his personal brand or, in the case of candidates the question is more often what's his campaign brand?

"Seattle's light rail guy" or the "advocate for smart environmentally friendly transportation solutions in metro areas"? What's the winning brand? The first is a one-issue local candidate with no potential for brand expansion and enhancement. The second is a potential author, speaker, consultant and commentator of regional or even national stature. It's the same guy with the same skills; just a better presentation.

And, as you will see in a later section – a nationally branded candidate has an immense advantage over a local candidate in local elections. This candidate is more powerful if elected because he carries the stature of his national brand, his author status and Leading Voice branding. If he doesn't get elected he still has a book deal, lucrative consulting opportunities and paid speaking engagements until the next election if he wants to run again.

Our message: as you're building the foundation for your brand, expand your thinking and create room for a powerful personal brand to grow.

MARKETING YOUR POWERFUL PERSONAL BRAND

Marketing your personal brand is the next element of the fame formula. Some people have the wrong idea about what's included in marketing; their definition is something tacky involving sales gimmicks and loud pitch men. They confuse marketing with selling and no one likes selling. If you do your marketing correctly and pay attention to the rest of the fame formula, others will always do your selling for you.

In our fame formula, marketing is a huge concept but in essence it's the process where you take an idea of how to fill a need in the market and convert that idea into a packaged product or service that is then presented to the buyers in the market. In this case that packaged product is Brand You and the value you offer.

As you put together a marketing plan for your personal brand we want you to always remember that what you're doing is creating interest in and demand for your services.

Personal marketing is initially about packaging the role you've defined for yourself in the most appealing manner.

Your personal marketing plan will also require you to research your playing field to spot the leading personal brands and to research their message, their marketing, and their effectiveness. You'll want to look for a gap in the market that your skillset and interest allows you to fill.

Once you've defined the market, or what we keep referencing as the playing field, you'll need to design your approach to positioning yourself to capture the market. There are quite a few common strategies used by the Super Elite personal brands that you'll find throughout Fame 101 but your effort will be to use those examples to design a specific marketing plan of your own.

Personal marketing is thus, just as with personal brand strategy and publicity, one necessary element of the fame formula. The personal brand you define must be packaged and rolled out to the market you define; but there's one more element in our recipe for fame. We call it Personal Evolution.

PERSONAL EVOLUTION –
YOUR BRAND MUST CONSTANTLY EVOLVE

Every element of the fame formula so far has a big element of fun; and thus it's easy to skip over the final element of the fame formula because it's disguised as work. Publicity can be a blast if you let yourself enjoy it – feature articles, morning talk shows, radio interviews and the rest.

Creating a powerful personal brand is also a very entertaining experience. The process requires you to lock down your dream life and the role you will use to grow into that life. What human endeavor could be more exciting? Personal marketing, with all the micro decisions that go into packaging and rolling out Brand You, is an amusing process also.

The thing to watch out for here is that all these cool activities can divert you from a critical activity: Personal Evolution. We're not talking here about some New Agey concept of consciousness raising or achieving some higher plane of existence; no, it's something much simpler and absolutely necessary for your fame effort.

Personal Evolution is constant continuous learning. Other than the 50 faces you see on the mind-candy supermarket magazines, the successful famous people in every field understand that while being visible is valuable you must be able to back it up with smarts, with talent, with ability.

Tiger Woods practices golf every single day. He has a personal trainer to keep himself in world class shape; he studies the courses he will play, newly developed equipment and strategies of other players. No one sees this day after day, week after week professional development that goes on behind the scenes.

We see Tiger effortlessly addressing the course at a major tournaments. We see him marrying a supermodel. We see him doing Buick ads for some insane amount of endorsement money but we don't see the daily activities that built his brand and enable him to maintain it.

Now with Brand Tiger in mind, and he's a great one to emulate as it is a billion dollar brand, take a look at the big players in any field including your own. They may not be the smartest, the best looking, or the most clever but every single one understands and is committed to Personal Evolution.

Cadillac makes a great car but they have an R & D (Research and Development) lab that is working on evolving this iconic vehicle to its next level. Where would this brand be if they just accepted the 2010 model as a great car and never evolved a new one? The same thing applies to brand you. You must have your own virtual R & D lab and you must learn, train and practice your profession.

If you are an insurance broker seeking fame the rules are the same as with Tiger and his golf game. You need to constantly study the new products and services in the industry but to be a real player and have a shot at the elite 1% you need a broader view of your personal evolution. Insurance is a financial product so you should learn how it fits among other financial products and then learn more than your competitors about those other products.

Then, as part of the evolutionary process you must constantly study the big picture; and a lot of fame is about the relevant big picture, which is the economy and business environment. So you're not just taking continuing education courses for insurance brokers, although those are good and necessary; you're consistently reading general business magazines from Fast Company to Forbes.

Then, you are attending seminars on collateral fields as diverse as marketing, social media technologies, or taking a few high-end business courses at the local university. You're attending lectures presented by any business leader of repute and you're reading the high end business authors. This is the personal evolution we're talking about to build power brand you.

The list of evolutionary activities is different for every field but you get the idea. Smart is cool, up to date is necessary, broad-expertise is necessary; all of these concepts go into the fame element Personal Evolution. Don't get diverted by the fun parts of building fame; we've seen many fame seekers stumble on the fame path because they thought they could skip this crucial element of learning and constant professional development.

It's not necessarily the most fun element of fame but it is absolutely necessary. You need the big-picture knowledge base to do a great interview and you need the out-of-your-industry connections to spot new opportunities for brand expansion. Constantly evolve; it's the key to fame.

THAT'S THE FAME FORMULA

If you are reading only one chapter of Fame 101, this was likely the one that drew your attention. Everyone wants a formula for success and you now know the path. It's the precise formula that made Picasso possible, Princess Diana the most notable royal of a century, and put the established leader of your industry in that position.

But here's the real secret: just having the formula isn't enough. We've got a great recipe for making bread but we'll starve unless we do something with it. Okay, this is a weak kitchen-analogy (unless of course you're the next Rachael Ray) but what we want to point out is that you must go over all of the material in Fame 101 to see how it all works and to learn the keys to making each element of the fame formula work for you.

Building, marketing, and publicizing a personal brand is a lot of work and it will take at least a year before you start to see real results; but, the rewards are nothing less than achieving your maximum personal potential and all the life-perks that you get when you make that happen. You're holding the fame formula in your hand – use it.

THE CELEBRITY NEXT DOOR

ANYONE CAN
HAVE FAME

· ·

"In a country of equals, some people are certainly more 'equal' than others. They have that indefinable something; powerful personal branding defines that something. The exciting thing is that anyone can become a compelling brand in their profession."

—Jay Jessup

· ·

YES, WE SAID ANYONE

Fame isn't just for rock stars - anyone can have it. That's right; anyone. We know it's true because creating and monetizing fame is what we do and what we've done for a decade. If you apply the fame formula you can become a celebrity actor, veterinarian, baker, dentist, florist or horse breeder. It would even be possible to become a celebrity assistant, security guard or librarian.

We're not saying it's easy. You can't do it without work; it takes a lot — more if you're starting from scratch but anyone can get there. Fame comes about from applying a formula that we have distilled down to its essence: Personal Branding + Publicity + Brand You Marketing + Personal Financial Development + Brand Longevity Strategies.

We'll look at each of these elements in their own chapters but for now, just remember fame is a formula and it works for anyone. Let's look at some logical fame applications where the benefits, and the beneficiaries, are readily apparent: candidates for office, attorneys, doctors, authors and entertainers. If you fall within one of these categories you see the results of your peers applying the fame formula daily.

They're the winning candidates, the lawyers who get the best cases, the doctors with their own television show or product line, best-selling authors, and entertainers who have risen above the casting call crowd and now get parts because of the strength of their personal brand.

Now if you're a fourth grade teacher in Kansas City you readily understand how fame applies to these traditionally very visible and highly trained people but you may not see how it can apply to your position. The fame that we know is readily within your grasp might not be visible to you but believe us, it's there.

We'll close out this chapter demonstrating exactly how the fame formula can put the spotlight on this Midwest educator, deliver to her a high-impact national platform and the access, power and money that comes from the right kind of celebrity. For the rest of you, the teacher is just an example; the point is that anyone can have fame. Let's start with candidates for public office.

CANDIDATES: NATIONALLY KNOWN LOCAL CONTENDERS AND LOCALLY KNOWN NATIONALS

Candidates with the best name recognition have a built in substantial advantage in any election. Ask any political operative and they'll tell you that the simple yard signs you see everywhere during campaigns make all the difference in elections. Even the placement of candidate signs has become an art; campaign managers care little about one voter having a sign in their yard while putting Vote for Tom placards on each side of a busy four way intersection is a big win.

Our fame strategy for candidates takes the reasoning behind yard signs to the next level. If you accept the premise that simple name recognition makes a big difference in elections, our position, which proves itself time and again, is that very high-visibility candidates will win the preponderance of elections. Voters will recognize not only the name but can also have positive feelings about the candidate's personal brand.

We help candidates get elected by building a Powerful Personal Brand for them and starting the plan at least a year and sometimes even two, before an election. You can do some things in just six months but if you're a thoughtful candidate who wants to maximize their chances you will start building your platform well in advance.

To avoid confusion we should note here that when we reference Platform, as defined elsewhere herein, we do not mean the policies a candidate intends to advance. Rather, in our world a platform is the sum total of a branded person's websites, professional activities, books, articles, speeches and the rest.

If the message of this section is that a candidate should use a fame plan to maximize her personal brand well in advance of an election, let's look at several fame elements to see if they add value to the campaign. Would a candidate with a best selling book be more likely to win an election than someone without such an advantage? President Kennedy would have said yes with his Profiles in Courage and his losing opponent, Richard Nixon would agree. As a matter of fact, the losing candidate later penned some 18 books and by the way, was elected president himself.

Do you think a candidate who kept a good database of his "fans" over a few years would have an advantage? Absolutely yes. Would the candidate who consistently takes the time over a year or two to participate in social media, to understand its power, and to build a following be more likely to win an election? President Obama would say yes as would every politician with future aspirations who is now racing to be the next big blogger.

Finally, fame encompasses something that candidates have known for a long time; great messaging, excellent presence, and a home run speech are uber powerful in an election and usually determinative. Each of these fame elements can be developed and perfected. Almost anyone who is willing to work at it can become "that" candidate. A little media training or a professional speech writer can take you a long way.

Fame is the common element among winning candidates. Are you running for office? Embrace the celebrity concept; your opponent could discover it first and outplay you before you even register as a candidate. Do you want to be president? Is it realistic? Perhaps not, but someone gets elected and it's usually the one with a great personal brand, so why not develop yours?

Should you despair because you're an out of work actor with sudden political aspirations? Governor Schwarzenegger or President Reagan would likely tell you to hang in there. Do you need to start out with a powerful Washington DC base in order to succeed in national politics? Ask a Georgia peanut farmer or an Arkansas Governor; at least a couple of them will tell you there is another path to elected office.

LAWYERS: WHILE THE REST ARE LUNCHING, THE PLAYERS ARE LAUNCHING

Some years ago we overheard a conversation between two successful businessmen at an upscale private club. Under the guise of complaining they were engaging in some subtle one-upmanship. While they were seemingly complaining, in actuality they were bragging. One fellow protested "My lawyer is killing me. He charges $400 an hour!" The other responded "Mine too. She charges about the same but she's the One Who Wrote the Book."

If you're a professional and harbor any doubts about the applicability of the fame strategy to your circumstance, remember that conversation and it's just one illustration of how some notoriety can enhance your brand value and income. We can promise you that no one will question your fees, although not everyone will be able to afford them, if you become a best selling author in the field.

America's law schools are turning out insane numbers of lawyers and most of them picture themselves in two thousand dollar suits arguing for the rights of a high paying client in the United States Supreme Court. The Lamborghini, arm candy, and major crib will soon follow. And those are just the new lawyers. The older lawyers who survive in the profession dream of judgeships, the ten million dollar case or the celebrity client.

The top one percent of the legal profession has all of those perks or at least as many of them as they want. They might own a winery, contribute to the arts and seem to have an endless supply of high-paying clients. Are these super lawyers the ones who came out at the top of their class at some amazingly elite law school? Do they have the best legal minds? The answer is typically No to these questions.

In our consultancy we get to meet quite a few lawyers as we do seminars at law firms wanting to leap to the top one percent of their fields. They absolutely cannot figure out how another lawyer, who isn't as smart or connected, effortlessly gathers most of the best clients. They see their less talented contemporaries featured in the society columns, getting book deals, and getting short listed for judicial appointments.

Here's the difference: the "lucky" ones understand and apply the fame formula. Most don't even realize they're doing it but the most successful, the ones with the big benefits that last a lifetime, completely get it. They invest in publicity; they plan their professional activities to operate in a synergistic manner and pay constant attention to their personal brand.

Does this mean they're overly concerned about their image, alerting the media every time they buy a new shirt? Do they have crazy big egos? Absolutely not. The fame formula is not superficial; it's a process where you make certain strategic personal and professional decisions resulting in a solid base from which you can gather all that life has to offer. It's simply smart personal branding, smart marketing, and appropriate publicity: typically backed by some cool technology and social media.

Did you watch CNN this morning? America's love affair with experts covers lawyers too. I can almost guarantee there was at least one talking head attorney, a CNN legal correspondent, giving an opinion on a case he or she knew nothing about other than what they'd seen on CNN. It seems kind of foolish when you look at the phenomenon from this angle but that's the way it is.

If you want to be *the* attorney in your town, your state or even the country, roll out your own fame plan: write a book, give the right speech to the right audience, get some media attention and use it wisely. Fame will give you a television show, the most desirable clients or even a Senate seat – take your pick or make your own wish list for fame to deliver.

DOCTORS: HARRIED PHYSICIAN OR COMPOSED VISIBLE PROFESSIONAL?

For some reason you feel better having your appendix taken out by the doctor who did the same for the Secretary General of the United Nations. This "gut" feel makes no sense; logic would suggest you'd rather have a local specialist who has done the surgery thousands of times but logic doesn't apply in our world. In the country that puts the famous on pedestals, the highest one is reserved for the celebrity doctor and the celebrity doctor is the one we want.

How do we know that celebrity doctors are among the hottest of hot? Consider that a full 20% of drama TV shows are doctor related – the finale of ER had a higher rating than the Super Bowl. There's even an increasing percentage of Reality TV focused on the fame pertaining to the savviest of MDs. Beverly Hills Boobs and the doctor who creates them delivers high ratings as dissatisfied women expose all on television for a chance to get a new pair from the guy who did Jen's.

Where did the boob guy come from? How did he get the show? After all it's a fairly simple surgery and there is no artistry beyond deciding between 34 C and 36 B. The doc with his own television show understood fame from before he got out of medical school. He learned the business side of fame; where the money is. In the case of Reality TV he's not making the money from the cosmetic surgeries, although the value of his practice is likely skyrocketing because of the exposure, more likely he's producing the show and getting the ad and syndication revenues.

But there's more to his success than business math. He's developed the other elements of fame also – his messaging is great, his appearance is correct for the role and his lifestyle supports this very same role. I promise he doesn't drive to the studio in a Ford Taurus and he likely dines quite publicly at the latest Los Angeles eatery with his magnificently boobed clients. What's more, the celeb-conscious restaurateur likely comps his meal while the maitre'd tips the paparazzi off to the photo op. Fame feeds on fame and so do the famous.

The special brand of fame available to doctors isn't focused entirely on cosmetics, although it's certainly fun for television viewing. Diet doctors are huge; no pun intended. After dating and relationships, dieting is the top category of best selling books. It seems we can't get enough of them; these doctors have great images and desirable book titles: It's Not Your Fault Diet, the Monte Carlo Diet, the Donut Diet or whatever the title. America will give the MD author fame and everything that comes with it.

What does all this have to do with you; a family practitioner in Austin, Texas? Everything. While the cosmetic and diet docs are playing on a crowded fame field, there are many additional niche spots available. A cancer doc can achieve fame and celebrity, as can a generalist. Even a good research doc can become famous as celebrity scientists are the next big thing. The only guy who might have a tough time is the proctologist but with the right packaging even he can rise to the top.

The word "wellness" tested very highly in a recent medical advertising study; it's something we all want. Of course we want to lose another 5% of our body weight and everyone would like a cosmetic redo but at the end of the day we all want to live longer and healthier. The doctor who can most visibly offer the key to wellness will get the television coverage, top speaking engagements and biggest book deal.

For the doctor in Austin? It's just a matter of getting visible in Silicone Gulch with the Texas Diet.

AUTHORS: BEST SELLER STATUS ISN'T ABOUT THE BOOK

Authors have a terrific tool to leverage for fame – a book or, even better, a series of books. In this section we're not talking about how and why to become an author as part of your fame platform; rather we are looking at how an obscure author can become famous. J. K. Rowling is the most successful author of the decade holding half of the top ten spots on the best-selling 100.

Ten years ago she was living in her car and now she's on top of the world. Her writing is great and her plots are terrific but it's the fame machine that differentiated her from another 100 authors who are just as good, but still unknown. Merchandising deals don't just happen; a generation of kids wanting to be Harry or Hermione from her books happened using the same fame formula as the Beatles used 30 years earlier.

Rowling, and ultimately her publisher, built an unbeatable team of publicists, business managers, marketing pros, buzz people, and street teams. For the uninitiated, buzz people are hired to plant seeds and start conversations in the social media arena, while street teams focus on a geographic location to deliver bodies to events. They're the people who put the rock show posters on telephone polls and get the word out that J.K. will be at the local Barnes & Noble at noon tomorrow.

The J.K. miracle is an example of the hard and fast publicity push surrounding a new book or a movie and how it can deliver fame. At the other end of the author fame strategy is Jack Canfield, known to most of us as the Chicken Soup for the Soul guy. By every measure he's a big success with some 20 titles in the Chicken Soup series but he's making similarly large amounts of cash by managing his fame platform.

Canfield is probably the steadiest and smartest fame builder out there today. Since the first Chicken Soup book he has constantly sought out radio shows to guest on, often doing several in one day. It's much easier for him now as everyone knows about him and his books but at the beginning he was doing every second and third tier city radio show he could get booked on. A show might sell one book or ten; now he does the bigger markets and sells a hundred or a thousand books every time he does a thirty minute guest appearance.

The fame concept for authors doesn't stop here and Jack Canfield is a pro at the other ways to build and monetize a fame platform. Every week he has one or two or five paid speaking engagements that increase his visibility, sell more books and certainly make money.

So fame building for authors is a long term multi-faceted thing where occasionally you get on a serious roll around a book launch or a movie but most of the time it's pounding it out one speech, article or radio show at a time. And what are the fame benefits to an author beyond the immediate income? If an author steadily builds a platform and a powerful personal brand it will be ever easier to sell their next book to a publisher as well as to their increasing fan base.

ACTORS, MUSICIANS AND OTHER ENTERTAINERS: IT'S WAY MORE THAN TALENT

You would think that people in the entertainment business, even if they're just starting, would grasp and embrace the concept of fame and celebrity faster than anyone. It's just not true, as we've learned from years of helping people in the business rise from obscurity by building their fame platform.

Garage bands, relatively new actors and others believe that fame is for others and that all there is to it is the red carpet stroll. It's one of the most rewarding aspects of our profession to see someone completely light up when they realize that fame is just a formula, anyone can have it, and that it's a matter of work. The concept kills the idea that fame only happens serendipitously.

For musicians, who gets the record deals? Which band is booked in the best clubs? And what group gets invited to tour as the opening act for a nationally known band? It's the same as with the lawyers, doctors or anyone else who has fame: it's the one seen on television, the one with the consistent social media strategy, and it's the one who keeps track of their fans by building a list so they can have 200 people show up in two hours at a local club.

The strategy is the same for new actors or for others who have had some number of modest roles over the years. The right date for an industry event with paparazzi capturing the moment, an interview in a non-industry magazine, involvement with the right charity, a key talk show appearance or a strategic appearance in a possibly-hot new indie film all can take an actor to the next level of fame.

Thereafter an exercise book, a keynote at a county Republican women's event, or even a product line will keep up the visibility and make an actor that much more desirable at the next casting opportunity. Of course with each of these there's an increase in sources and amounts of income; yet another benefit of building a fame platform. In the fame business everything operates synergistically.

Actors, musicians and other entertainers don't need to already be 'hot' to get the benefits of fame. Rather it's those who understand, build and use fame to get hot who are the most likely to make it in the business. And of course the entertainment industry rewards the famous in many magnificent ways. That is why there are so many people trying to break into the business and why it is vitally important to your success to use the fame formula to get past the clutter to join the top 1% of the profession.

TEACHERS: MISS NELSON HEADS FOR THE OSCARS

How does all this fame talk apply to Miss Nelson, a fourth grade teacher at Jimmy Carter Elementary in Kansas City? In a country that too frequently measures professional worth by paycheck size, a fourth grade teacher is pretty far down the value scale and unfortunately self perception usually follows. If we went to Miss Nelson and told her she could be famous in a year, could have an immense impact on the world and earn two million dollars in 48 months, her life experience would cause her to tell us we're crazy.

Are those goals unrealistic for this situation? Do you have to be a doctor, lawyer, big-time candidate or author to grasp life's silver ring? Absolutely not; fame can be created and fame can put Miss Nelson on top of her profession. It can be her key to the top 1% of income earners in the United States. That's what is great about fame – anyone can have it and anyone can use it to achieve their dreams.

Don't take our word for it; let's look at a fame path for Miss Nelson and keep in mind there are several such options open to her. You'll see how each fame element comes together throughout the course of this book but for now let's simply make her famous.

We think there is drama, the movie kind not the gossip kind, in every profession from rice farmer to controller and spotting it is step one toward fame. So what is it in Miss Nelson's profession that could capture an audience's attention? Easy answer – Miss Nelson has the future of our country and possibly the world in her hands. From September to June, every year, she has an immense impact on the lives of thirty children.

Now many fourth grade teachers simply see their job as taking a group of kids from third grade academic skill levels to readiness for the rigors of fifth grade. Not Miss Nelson; she knows that she also can plant the seeds of greatness in each of these children. In just nine months she can use the latest in educational theory to expose her charges to a bigger world and give them tools to thrive in society. Isn't that what education is all about?

Miss Nelson seeks out the latest research on elementary education; what works and what doesn't as well as what's next. She knows the Gates Foundation is doing some heavy work on redefining education; she researches what they're doing, connects with them and studies other exciting elementary education initiatives.

She writes an article on the exciting things she's learning: multi-sensory teaching techniques, interactive study techniques, and other really exciting futuristic strategies to live up to the enormity of the responsibility the school board and 30 some parents have placed in her hands. Sally Nelson starts a blog; note the brand perception strength of Sally Nelson vs Miss Nelson. She studies social media and connects with other teachers around the world.

Sally starts an online community of elementary school teachers interested in multi-media education and learns more from them. All this time she's taking notes about what she's learning and speculating on what else might be possible to engage the minds of her fourth grade class. Her binder full of notes starts filling up and then someone like us points out she has enough material for a book: Sally Nelson becomes an author.

She uses the exact strategies found in each chapter of this book and soon she's an author, a speaker, a consultant to school boards across the country; she seeks input from other progressive educators to develop a model curriculum designed to make fourth grade the most meaningful experience possible. She copyrights the material and licenses it to schools everywhere.

Sally Nelson will need to pay attention to her image, messaging, publicity and other fame elements along the way but, properly executed, her fame plan can put her in the top one percent of U.S. income earners. She can build a fame platform from which she can have a broad impact on the future of the country. Or, Miss Nelson can spend her days teaching the kids at Jimmy Carter Elementary how to make Thomas Jefferson stickers. Do the kids not deserve more? Can a fourth grade teacher create and use fame? Yes she can, using any of several fame paths open to her. And so can anyone.

FAME 101

YOUR FAME
FOUNDATION
THE PLATFORM

"Fame separates you from the group – you become
an icon; it lets you live and work in a place of power."
—Jay Jessup

A PLATFORM – THE KEY TO SYNERGISTICALLY GROWING YOUR BRAND

We hear from fame seekers every week who are excited about going on television for the first time, an upcoming article in their local newspaper featuring their business, or a speech at their industry convention the next month. They tell us that this is their big break and it's certain that they'll be an everlasting success from this point forward. Some even start planning on how to handle the paparazzi.

If you've made it this far reading Fame 101 you know what's really going to happen; they'll get their moment and their friends will tell them how fabulous they sounded on the morning show, how the article was terrific and that their speech was one of the best ever. But, and you see it coming, no new income opportunities will be generated. The momentary celebrity will quickly fade and this person slides back into mediocrity never knowing exactly why their big break didn't happen.

That story happens all the time; almost as often as there are sections in the newspaper, guest slots on AM-TV, and speaker spots on the program at every industry's annual event. What's tragic for all these unborn stars is that the result could have been very different. A television appearance could have launched their new book, an article could have been leveraged into fifty more and their speech could have been used to drive audience members to a business website for more information and ultimately sales.

There's just one difference between the people who launched and the ones who stalled; the winners in this game had a platform and you must have one too. No, we aren't talking about a political platform where a candidate outlines the goals, principles, and policies of her candidacy. Rather, a platform in the fame world is the sum total of your websites, speaking engagements, professional activities, media appearances, books, media kit, articles, messages, social media connections, charitable associations, organizations you control or influence, your fan list (yes a dentist or farmer can have fans) and other elements. Your platform is your fame foundation.

To understand the benefits of having an in-place platform consider the following illustrative scenario: prior to your speaking engagement you made a deal with the conference organizers to have a complimentary booth in the convention hall to present your professional offerings (product, service or whatever) and also delivered a complete media kit with obsessively concise compelling copy describing yourself, the profession you're in and your differentiators.

Even prior to the convention people are reviewing the program and your speech looks like a must-attend because you delivered to the organizers a presentation title that absolutely sizzles and the best possible brief description of yourself. Everyone is looking forward to your speech, and talking about it, before getting to the event.

Then when they sit down in the room they find on their chairs a Meet Dr. Megan Smythe glossy 8.5" by 5.5" card with a brief overview of your professional activities, a couple of your best qualifying bullets, the day's subject and most important, a way to connect with you after the event.

This connection opportunity is typically your website which, because you understand the importance of a platform, you have had it created to present the best possible you and your professional offerings online.

YOUR OWN PERSONAL PLATFORM

Wow, we just learned how the speaking element of your platform, when combined with the website element, creates an opportunity to maximize every speaking engagement. You made a quality advance impression with well-thought-out materials forwarded to conference organizers which they used, word for word, in their marketing of the event. As attendees were looking forward to your presentation their impression was reinforced by a powerful personal marketing piece awaiting them at their chair or table spot.

Your Big Speech was interlaced with language which would drive listeners to your website, remembering they have that URL in the materials already in several places, and some number of those people are sufficiently intrigued to go to your site, find out more and then call you for services.

You can stop reading now if all you're interested in is tripling the business development aspects of speaking engagements; but you'll never have fame – possibly you might have fame lite but never the life changing, world impacting, powerfully publicized personal branding we're offering you in your reading of Fame 101.

What's missing? The rest of your platform! Simply because you've just implemented a strategy that only a small percentage of speakers are able to do well, you mustn't be satisfied. Merely adequate satisfaction is the enemy of fame because you get lazy as things are better than they were. You must constantly be looking for things to get better and better, and even incredibly amazing; that's how you get and keep fame.

So let's look at how someone who truly understands fame could expand the above fact situation with a broader platform. To start out you'll read in Fame 101 that you must have a book (don't worry, you'll see just how easy it is to make that happen). If the above referenced speaker had a book, which was tied generally to her professional offerings, then the advance materials could have a shared focus on the marketing of that book as well as leveraging the speaker's Author Status.

A great publicist could use the book to entice one or more members of the media to either cover the speech or use the speech, plus the book to capture a guest spot on that city's morning show because an author is in town to give a presentation. The media always likes someone from out of town more than a local; it doesn't make sense but it's a fact of media life.

The television appearance could generate more advance excitement by conference attendees who see you on the morning show while having their pre-event breakfast; they in turn will whisper to those around them before the speech that they saw the speaker on the morning show thus giving the speaker the credibility that we all give to people we see on television.

It's also a pretty great personal brand builder to have the media in visible attendance at your speech or interviewing you on camera five minutes before going on stage. We had People Magazine and ABC News (national) at a small town event a few months ago (plus some regional media outlets) and the community is still abuzz as the event made national news.

The conference booth, which you got for free because you're "famous" and have a platform, can have your assistant selling books in advance of your presentation or at least handing out postcards promoting your speech. At this point your platform has delivered to you a standing room only crowd of people who already think highly of you and they're all excited to hear your message.

Your message rocks because you've spent a ton of time working on the best possible speech, although the way you deliver it is almost like you're speaking extemporaneously. You've practiced in front of a video camera and other audiences; you might have even spent some time with a voice coach. You have captured the sound of intelligence and you never say "Uh" or "Um"; you don't ramble and when you're done you stop rather than trying to fill time and your conclusion leaves the audience wanting to know more.

In the back of the room there's a book signing waiting for you so you pick up book sale income as well as your presentation fee. Your books and your presentation and your media appearances all reinforce the message that you're interesting and whatever service or product you sell will be more desirable because it's part of the Big Personal Brand you've created.

An increased number of these people will visit your website and sign up for your newsletter because they want to be part of the community which has you at its center.

We could go on and on and on, as could your brand if, and only if, you have a platform to feed all this activity while capturing and maximizing the personal benefits. So, what's the lesson here? One element of a platform is a great career enhancer; a complete platform with all elements in place is a fame creator – it's Brand You, brilliantly packaged and presented to the market.

We just covered a few fame platform elements here; you'll find the others throughout this book. The big idea is that your platform creates that Air of Celebrity for you and has foundational elements in place to gather all the benefits that flow toward you as a Leading Voice of your field.

YOUR NEW BEST FRIEND SHOULD BE A SPIDER

Some people we meet have great fame potential; they already have the look, some presence and one or more cool mediagenic things going on but they are in a complete stall while seeming incredibly busy. They have finished half of their book (it's on the table), they are members of several associations (but they're not maximizing the benefits), they have an adequate website (but is "adequate" ever sufficient for fame?), their professional life is filled with mostly-finished projects (but "who's got time"?), they might have many diverse clients and their personal life is busy too, because they're interesting nice people.

Does any of this sound familiar? Many people are crazy-busy these days; they have so much going on they couldn't add even one more thing, like organizing all these activities, without a meltdown. The tough thing is that this type of person (and you are likely one of them if you're interested in this book), just knows that they are within sight of achieving something big; but, they can't identify or achieve that thing because they're too close with no big picture vision and they're too busy.

They know that each of their activities and opportunities could be leveraged to deliver even more and better results. But, there's no time; and they're frustrated because they know this. In our opinion these people all hit a defining moment, especially when they learn about fame.

They can either continue in their too-busy professional life, keeping ahead of much of their competition by the sheer force of their busyness or they can take a leap forward into the exceptional life that fame can deliver. Step one in making this transition from marginal-return insane busyness to a synergistic high-leverage high-impact fame machine is creating what we call your spider.

What a spider does is create a one-page graphic representation of your most efficient and effective professional life. It enables you to think strategically and make effortless decisions about which activities to focus on, which to invest more time and money in, and which to drop completely.

This one page graphic, we call a spider. So take out a piece of paper and let's quickly do your first draft; many of our clients have told us this is a life-transforming experience. Maybe that's true but we promise it's at least professionally valuable and very cool fame-wise so go ahead and start by drawing a two inch by two inch circle in the middle of the page.

FIGURE 1

In the center of this circle write the word Brand (Your Name); we'll pretend you're Bob, so the very center of this sheet is Brand Bob. That is now your focus; everything you do and all your professional activities are designed to build Brand You and deliver benefits (money and otherwise) to yourself. If there is an activity in your life that isn't building the brand or bringing you those benefits, drop it, at least for now.

This is the body of your spider. The next step is adding the legs. So draw eight legs; four on each side of the Brand You circle. Then at the end of each leg draw a two inch by two inch circle. Each of these circles is going to represent an activity that builds your brand and/or delivers benefits which again, are typically money-related.

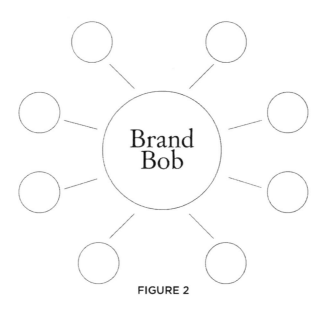

FIGURE 2

Everyone's spider is going to be different but there are many common elements, so for purposes of quick illustration let's fill out Bob's spider with the following (each is written in one of the new "leg" circles) assuming he's say, an attorney: Bob's Book, Personal celebrity website, Business website,

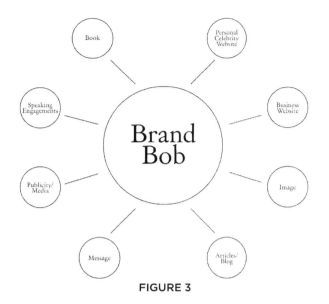

FIGURE 3

Speaking Engagements, Media Appearances/Publicity, Image, Message, and Articles/Blog.

As you go through the exercise of drawing your first spider draft, you will start the process of learning to focus on your brand. Every activity you undertake should have this one goal – enhance the value of Brand You. As we said, many people find creating this simple first draft spider an enormously freeing experience.

They have had so much going on for so long and they're so busy that their focus has been lost. They can't answer the question "Why am I doing this?" for any professional activity. With your spider you will always know why you're spending the time to write a book – it will enhance the value of your brand, help to bring you fame, and that will make your life easier. The same is true of every other element of your spider.

For instance, you can see why you're putting the time into building a speaking career – it will enhance the value of your brand, help to bring you fame, and that will make your life easier. Well, you can see what this is all about; your new best friend can be, and really should be, a spider.

ARACHNI-SYNERGY

If you're the typical fame seeker you will probably admit the value of creating your own personal spider but many people then tell us that they just don't have time to do these eight separate things. They say that although this graphic helps them focus, they're concerned that it just creates eight new things to think about and "There's no time." Nonsense.

Here's the beauty: a secondary benefit of creating this fame map is that it helps you synergize and leverage all your activities. What we mean by this is that every element of your spider/fame plan simultaneously benefits at least one other element with everything you do. For the simplest, quickest illustration consider what you learned above; speaking engagements also sell books. Dual benefits from one speech; this is leverage and this is the beginning of synergy.

Or, as another example, consider that a 1500 word article on a subject within your expertise takes quite a bit of time to write; however, once it's written, much of the same content can be adapted into three consecutive blog postings. Further, with a bit of cutting and pasting plus another two hundred words you could create a 400 word article, a 750 word article, 10 "tips" taken from the content, several press releases can be created and several cool bullets will come from the same material to be used in your presentations.

The same article, paraphrased, could be one half of a chapter in your next book – only nineteen more of these articles and there's a completed book. At the end of each and every article is a three or four line reference to you, your qualifications, your book, your website, and your professional practice; thus each of these many pieces you just created is a mini-advertisement.

Thus, one seemingly simple article promotes many other elements of your fame platform; it's just a matter of keeping this spider graphic in front of you at all times so you don't miss any opportunity for such synergy. While your competition stresses about completing a 1500 word article, skips the spider strategy, and anxiously rushes on to work on an upcoming speech, you're getting five times the benefits for the same amount of effort.

The bottom line is for you to understand that working harder and doing more professional activities than the next guy won't get you fame; it will just keep you tired. Fame comes from executing on a simple platform strategy and that approach is launched when you create your spider. You can stay focused on your goals and on achieving synergy because you will always have this single piece of paper which is nothing less than a roadmap to a phenomenal new professional life. Draw it; post it and follow your roadmap.

SPIDERS ON STEROIDS

Ideally now you have an eight-legged spider drawn on a sheet of paper with Brand You in the center. It makes sense and likely you have the best big picture grasp of your professional life that you've been able to achieve in years. If you're willing to put just a bit more thought into it you can take your spider to an even higher level of value.

Here's what we're talking about. To illustrate, let's start with a look at the circle labeled "Book". You know from reading Fame 101 that you must have a book and we even have an entire chapter itemizing the reasons for becoming an author. But, there are five principal activities in getting your book written and ultimately to market. To make your spider a more accurate representation of what you need to accomplish, let's list those on the graphic.

Start by drawing five outbound short lines from the Book circle and at the end of each list one task: title/outline, content, agent, publisher and marketing. There is really nothing else to be concerned about in making a

FIGURE 4

book happen and thus you needn't cloud your mind with anxiety that you might be missing something.

This is a key benefit of using a spider roadmap; no wasted time wondering what you could or should be doing or might have forgotten. Every necessary activity to build your brand is in one place. On this Book circle you know that books sell to a large extent by their title and to an equally important extent by their index. You know by looking at your expanded spider that you must check off this Create Title and Index activity before you'll have a book. The same is true with getting an agent; you won't get a real book deal without one and we believe self-publishing will brand you as an amateur.

But that's for another chapter, for now you know you must get an agent and won't have a book on the market until you've accomplished that task. With that referenced on your spider, that's another thing you needn't worry about missing; you'll need to put some time into securing an agent. The same is true for creating the content that will become your book and the other element to becoming an author is creating and executing a marketing plan to supplement your publisher's efforts. Those are the sub legs of your spider as relates to your book.

Another circle is your celebrity website which will have a media room, a video element, your blog…we could go through a whole spider sample here to demonstrate that each leg of the spider will have from three to five activities of their own and they should be listed next to their respective circles. However, you'll develop a more effective roadmap/spider if you go through the process yourself with each leg applying to your own personal brand.

You can see the concept. The next step is keeping your own draft spider nearby while you complete Fame 101. While you're reading and as your personal plan develops, add each To Do to your spider. By the end of the book you will have a precise roadmap to fame, specifically as it applies to your own brand. This might well be the most valuable take-away from Fame 101 – your fame platform spider.

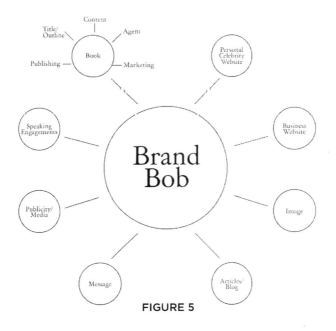

FIGURE 5

ALL SPIDERS ARE NOT CREATED EQUAL

We know you've got a lock on using spiders to create your personal road-map to an iconic personal brand and the resulting fame, but there is a risk here we should address. Whenever a complicated or powerful concept, like your fame foundation, is reduced to a formula or one-page graphic, there is a risk of relying too much on the structure as presented in an example.

To avoid this risk we want you to make sure you're listing, on your spider, the fame elements that apply to you – not simply those we used as illustrations. Certainly most everyone will have a book and do some speaking but there are other elements that might be unique to your profession, e.g., for an actor a demo reel/headshot as well as securing an agent are strategic imperatives and an actor's spider will have extra focus on those items.

Below are five additional circles for you to consider as examples to keep you thinking about which are most important in building Brand You. We discuss each of these in some detail throughout Fame 101, but for now consider each of the following as examples of other fame foundation elements:

An Association – If you're a florist in New Hampshire, garden guy in Louisiana, or a political consultant in Washington DC, you should consider founding an association. We cover the many reasons and benefits a bit later on but the essential idea is that you create an association for your industry, e.g., Northeastern United States Floral Association. It starts as little more than a web presence and may only have one member to start out; however, brand wise it's now the NUSFA and you're the executive director.

The media will be more receptive to your message and give you valuable air or print time as a seemingly impartial leader of a trade association rather than a florist, garden guy or political operative effectively pitching their own wares. We'll learn more of the possibilities later but for now consider the idea of creating an association and if it sounds right for your situation, add a spider leg.

Your Second Book – We give you a strategy for turning out books quickly and painlessly so don't panic now as we suggest you need to plan for your second book while you are still doing your first book. If you're on the fame path to a powerful place in your profession, it's our recommendation that you turn out a book every year to eighteen months. For most readers, especially if you're a great candidate for fame, you're now thinking you're just too busy.

Ignore that thought process for the moment and take a leap of faith with us based on a chapter in Fame 101 that can make a book happen quickly for anyone, no matter how busy. The point in this small section is to suggest that you include Book Two as a spider element or even Annual Book so you can plan several years in advance. There are many possible spider legs and for many people Book Two will be relevant, important, and valuable in your fame planning process.

Professional Education – This is a great spider leg and will apply to many Fame 101 readers. Whether you're a small business owner, an attorney or an actor, you have to keep developing and sharpening your skills. Fame isn't something handed to you without effort and you don't get to keep it without consistent effort. So, actors should constantly be taking new/different classes, attorneys should develop their skills from public speaking to the latest trial strategies, and business owners should be attending seminars on marketing or management.

Spin Off Products – Almost every fame area has some product possibilities. A business leader with a $20 book can also present very similar material as a $100 audio CD set, a $299 DVD course or as a $400 per hour consulting project. The concept of spin off products or services is limitless so if you believe there's a place on your platform to develop these additional revenue sources, go ahead and add a leg to your spider.

Online Magazine – We all know the power of the media; it can be your brand's best friend and help you in some amazing ways. However, you'll see in other chapters that it is a constant struggle to stay in the media so, given time and resources, many people become their own media source. By this we mean going one step beyond blogging and actually put together an online periodical.

It can be fairly simple with just a few articles each month, a reader community, and some modest advertising. In the alternative you can build a powerful online media outlet, sometimes referenced as an e-zine, where you control what gets published, who gets attention and more. Many books are written on this subject but for now, just accept the concept and add a spider leg if this is an area of interest.

An association, your second book, continuing education, spin-off products or an online magazine are terrific elements to add to your spider but remember they're just examples. The value of your spider is determined by how well you customize it for your specific situation. So to assure maximum value, put significant thought in finalizing each element of your spider.

YOUR PERSONAL FAME FOUNDATION

In a perfect world you're completing this chapter with a single piece of paper in hand that has a treasure map drawn in the center. If you're looking for fame and want to tip life's scales in your favor, you must have a fame foundation to define the necessary steps, keep them operating synergistically, and know what opportunities to focus on as well as which ones you should let fall by the wayside. Spider thinking maintains your focus on your own brand and your own goals.

Society's elite, who understand fame, are masters of multi-tasking, experts at creating synergy and they know when to leap and when to pass. Your spider is your guide and the resulting fame is your ticket to play. Keep this graphic at hand as you read on then post it in a prominent place next to your desk – it will deliver an organized, smarter professional life. Fame is the result of all these activities done concurrently and well; it's not an activity in itself – this is your platform.

EVERYONE LOVES AN AUTHOR
YOUR BOOK(S)

. . . .

"America has a love affair with experts; they're elevated to a higher social status. A legitimate book deal delivers the presumption of expert status like nothing else." —Jay Jessup

. . . .

AUTHOR STATUS IS A KEY ELEMENT OF FAME

What if your job was to get a very young candidate elected as President of the United States? You already have a pretty good sense of how it's done from what you've read so far in this volume about fame but you have to admit it could be a very tough task if your candidate was running against someone older and more experienced; in essence, more Presidential.

Now a presidential win for a seemingly too-young candidate isn't something that could be accomplished overnight; there would be some years of planning the right fame platform but a key element would be showing Gravitas (Latin word meaning – high seriousness). Are we talking about the Barrack Obama miracle? No, we're talking about someone even younger: the 35th President of the United States, John Kennedy – elected at age 43.

President Kennedy's candidacy and election were exceptionally well orchestrated. He was one of history's great leaders and we are in no way taking away from that but merely taking a behind-the-scenes look at this one fame element that helped him get elected. The element we want you to note here is Kennedy's book, *Profiles in Courage* which won a Pulitzer Prize in the biography category in 1957.

Profiles in Courage became a best seller, which you'll see later in this chapter is at least seventy five percent publicity and marketing, but what's important is it differentiated young Senator Kennedy from every other ambitious politician. The book gained him national recognition and the author status gave his brand the gravitas it needed to overcome the perception that he was too young to become president.

JFK led the way with this strategy and it is followed absolutely in elections today. Go to the bookstores in any presidential election year and you will see a book by every serious candidate – typically co-authored, but the candidate's name and face are on the cover. None that we've seen match the literary quality of Profiles in Courage, but that's not the point. A serious candidate must have a book; it's one of those items on every successful campaign checklist.

You are likely thinking this concept makes a great story but wondering what this has to do with building fame for an Amarillo attorney, a small business owner in Fresno, or even a local candidate for mayor? Our answer: Plenty. Writing and launching a book is one of the fastest ways for anyone to position themselves as an expert in their field. Author status creates a fantastic differentiator between you and your competition.

Think back to the conversation overheard about two lawyers and their large fees, one of which seemed justified because that attorney wrote the book.

Bottom line – be the One Who Wrote the Book. Author Status wins elections, captures the best clients, gets the Reality TV deals, garners media attention and makes you talked-about; always a key part of fame.

RULES & REALITIES OF BOOK DEALS

No matter what your profession, whether Hollywood actor or Tampa garden-guy building a personal fame platform, you obviously must have a book to capture the all-important Author Status we looked at in the previous section. But how does all that work? Where do the books you see in the stores come from and for that matter, why are some on the front table and others in the bargain bin?

First, we have to burst your bubble but don't be concerned because we offer the solution in this chapter. Here are the numbers: 95,000 books are published in the United States each year and those are the just the ones that got published. For each of these "lucky" ones there are a hundred manuscripts that never made it off the publisher's floor to even be read.

There are scores of books on How To Get Published but what they don't tell you is that 99% of the time publishers won't even look at your manuscript unless you have an agent. Agents in turn will not take you on as a client unless they're sure they can make enough money so that their typical fee of 15% of your royalties make their efforts worthwhile. There are not that many agents; all the good ones are inundated with manuscripts and requests for representation. Very few will take on first-time authors and then almost never without a personal referral.

The first exception to these publishing industry realities is for front-page celebrities offering a celebrity death, scandal or anything else that would headline in the grocery store checkout line sensationalist papers. In this category would be anyone with a ready book on Princess Di at her death, Anna Nicole Smith at her death, Monica Lewinsky or any other Clinton scandal person, Heath Ledger at his death, or Governor Sarah Palin at her launch.

Don't lose hope if you don't have the celebrity cachet to capture a book deal; there's a second exception to the publishing industry closed-door policy and you can become one of those exceptions without dying at a Hollywood nightclub or fooling around in the Oval Office. Agents and publishers will fall over themselves to sign an author with a strong platform.

The publishing industry is consolidating, or at least at the big publishing houses. They spend crazy marketing dollars on the big Anna Nicole, John Grisham, and presidential candidate titles as their principal profit generators, although they also launch many titles by new or second tier authors but do this with almost no marketing or publicity.

This is where the author platform comes in; agents will take on and publishers will offer a book deal to, any author who will, by virtue of their platform, sell thousands of books on their own. Yet, many authors believe their message is so important that people will stand in line to buy their book on the mating habits of North Wyoming wrens or some similarly world-changing topic.

There are a hundred variables but the bottom line is the same here, as it is throughout this fame volume: fame creates a community of people who are interested in you and your activities. If you will follow our counsel on identifying and profiling your fan base from Day One, you will have a verifiably ready market for your book, you'll get an agent, and be offered a book deal. It's All about personal fame.

TOO BUSY OR CAN'T WRITE? NO PROBLEM - A GHOST STORY

It is amazing how best selling non-fiction authors are able to run large businesses, campaign for President while maintaining a Senate seat, do interviews and appearances all over the country, produce a daily radio show and otherwise stay incredibly busy – *and still write a book a year.*

Actually, in a surprising number of cases they don't; write a book a year, that is. Another person or team helps with or completely does the writing. Meet the Ghostwriter. We have worked with many on behalf of our clients; some great, some adequate and a few others. A good ghostwriter typically has a very solid underlying formal education and a decade or more of real life experience.

Should you elect to go this route and select one for yourself it is our best advice that you look closely at this "real life experience" element of a ghostwriter's resume. Here's the reasoning: while a Yale graduate student in English might have phenomenal writing skills, odds are they've been holed up in academia for their entire adult lives and would miss many of the life realities that must be woven into any book to make it come alive.

The ghostwriter's job is to capture the authentic voice of their author-client, then gather and memorialize the author-client's ideas in an interesting and compelling manner. Many people think it's all really easy: "All she has to do is talk to me; I'll give her my important ideas and all she has to do is turn out 60,000 words!" You would be amazed at the people who don't appreciate the art form that is ghostwriting.

Some folks, when presented with the idea of a ghostwriter, believe it to be a tawdry business, much akin to plagiarism. What would you think if I told you that some of the biggest personal brands you see out there, who have five, ten, or twenty books to their credit, use ghostwriters? Even we were astounded at first when a high level executive at one of the world's most respected publishers shared that a very 'A' list faith-based author with many, many books to his credit had never put a pen to paper.

So, accept that the presidential candidate you voted for likely had a ghostwriter and it is part of platform building to achieve that author status. It will be up to you to decide the structure of your ghostwriting arrangement. Some authors give the ghostwriter a subject and title and order a sixty thousand word book.

Other authors, and we believe this the best course in many cases, work hand in hand with the ghostwriter for a couple of hours at a time with chapters going back and forth until complete: a reasonable joint effort. The next question is whether or not to share credit on the cover. Travel to any bookstore, check out the best sellers and you'll find many have the big brand SARA DOE and then in smaller font "with Jane Smith".

Or, pass on sharing the cover; the business-side here is that you just purchased some content from a commercial entity – the ghostwriter. It's yours; use it as you wish. It all comes down to what best fits for you.

The final questions and answers: Where do you get a ghostwriter? Personal referrals or online. Referrals are always better but online is fine if you follow up in detail with their references and review samples of their work. How much does a ghostwriter cost? We have seen anywhere from $10,000 to well over $60,000 and the pricing doesn't necessarily reflect the quality.

So, you can't write a book but need one for your fame platform? A quality ghostwriter may be the answer.

YOUR IDEAL SUBJECT; IT'S NOT WHAT YOU THINK

Everyone accepts they need a book to elevate their personal brand to the celebrity level but if you want to maximize the results you must have a home run book that appeals to a broad audience.

This sounds simple and most people have heard that everyone has a book inside them. However, our position is that a great majority of those books should stay there – inside and undiscovered. We hear from people all the time with the "most incredible divorce story", a collection of "break-out poetry", or the story of their lives from junior college to achieving the presidency of a regional ice cream company.

Some are offended when we have to tell them their divorce is not unique, there are perhaps three great poets in each generation and it probably isn't them, or that biographies only work for people who already have seriously big fame. This doesn't mean the divorcee, poet, or local executive can't get fame or turn out a home run book – the path just isn't with the subject matter for the book they have in mind.

Competing with the too-personal or too-local topics for a book is the Too-Specialized. We get to meet many remarkable people from every possible area of business, science, entertainment, sports and others. It seems that one thing they all have in common is very deep, very specialized knowledge in their niche. Most think this would be a great book subject.

Wrong. A lawyer who has spent a decade learning everything there is to know about intellectual property considerations for United States music industry companies doing business in former Soviet countries believes that this knowledge could make a definitive book on the subject. He's right that it could be definitive but it would be tough to find more than 100 people who would buy the book. Fame requires a broader audience.

Don't wait until you've written twenty or thirty thousand words to get a reality check on whether or not your book has a broad audience. Have a brutally honest friend or better an outsider in the book business let you know if you're on the right track.

Here's the thing: non-fiction authors have an elevated status in our society and when combined with our fame formula there is no limit to what you can accomplish. However, consider that your book title, for at least a year and perhaps for your life, will become inextricably tied to your brand and thus define your audience.

What is the best way to be sure of a home run book? Start with the title; books sell first by their title and your future speaking engagements will often be decided by the title of your book. Lots of people may buy it but only a small percentage will read it, an unfortunate reality in the non-fiction arena but you can thus see why the title becomes all important. Finally, many people will judge you by your book's title – these are your realities so put all your resources into that title.

Obama's *The Audacity of Hope*, Kennedy's *Profiles in Courage*, or even Martha Stewart's *Cooking School;* each title helped to identify and build these powerful brands in a big way. Also remember you are not writing the book to impress people in your own industry; for maximum brand power write for the audience you want to become your fans, clients or voters.

As a final note it never hurts for your title to have a built in media catch. If, when you read the title to someone, their head whips around in a double take or a quick smile comes to their face, you've got it right. What's your title?

NO TIME TO WRITE? EASY STEPS TO A FAST BOOK

There's nothing more intimidating to a would-be author than that first empty page or a blank computer screen. Every reason in the world why you can't write a book passes through your mind before you start. "I have four kids" "It's tax season" "Things are insane at the office" are among the many excuses and what's tough is they're all legitimate.

Everyone is busy these days, certainly the people who have a little something remarkable going on and could turn out a decent book. For all of you who see themselves in this category, there is hope and an easy answer.

Remembering we believe that you should already have at least a smoking hot mediagenic working title at this point, it's time to turn to the table of contents. Let's start filling up that blank computer screen in a painless way; don't let your subconscious worry you – you're not writing the book yet so your excuses can stay in place.

Type or write the title at the top of the page. Ideally it is a subject you know something about or can learn about with relative ease. Now start listing, in no particular order, different subsets of this subject that you could talk about for ten or twelve minutes.

For example, if you are planning on running for office in a year or two, your title would be something big and inspirational, but these subjects might logically be improving healthcare, boosting the economy, helping the homeless, enhancing education, ideas for smart transportation…

If you need either a jump start or if you go brain dead in the middle of making your list, go to any online bookstore and check out the table of contents on titles related to your subject. Others have been through this process before so there is no need to reinvent the wheel. We aren't suggesting you pirate their titles or ideas but this process does help to focus your thinking and inspire you as to what subsets of your subject are logical.

And think it through; determine what subjects are relevant. If you're doing a book on raising kids, what are the logical categories? Well, what you have to do with kids: feed them, dress them, school them, travel with them…

When you have somewhere between fifteen and twenty-five of these subjects, i.e., that you could talk about for ten to twelve minutes about, you have created a rough list of chapter titles. Certainly you'll rename, re-organize, and rethink all of these subjects, but you just took an important step in writing your book.

This effort likely took less than an hour and Surprise, you no longer are looking at a blank page – your book is now a work in progress. I don't care how busy you are; everyone has time to get this far. You might like this great strategy but maybe you're still worried about writing fifty or sixty thousand words and this will be tough with a "mostly" blank page.

Let your hopelessness rest a minute while I tell you about a best selling author we represent who's written 15 books (several best sellers), handles a heavy appearance schedule and yet always seems to have plenty of time to enjoy her ranch. One time when I called her she told me she was driving around in her classic Ford pickup "Writing her book".

When I asked how this was possible, she told me she takes one subject at a time, decides on 3 or 4 points she wants to make, then drives around while talking into a digital tape recorder. A typical 30 minute drive would net her about 3500 words; her assistant typed them up and the rest was just editing.

How does this apply to you? Easy. You already have the list of 20 or so topics you could talk about for twelve minutes. Pick one; come up with three or four points you'd like to make, then pick up your digital tape re-corder. Go for a walk in the park, drive someplace inspirational, or just sit in the kitchen and talk. Type up the results and you have a rough chapter for your book.

Take fifteen or twenty more drives and you have a rough draft of your book. Fine tune this strategy for what works in your life but, if you can devote 20 minutes a day, you can have a draft of your book sixty days from now. And, here's a secret: This is the exact formula many, many authors use to painlessly turn out a book a year. It's just that easy.

RECIPE FOR A BEST SELLER – PUBLICITY & PARTNERS

There is nothing as exciting as authoring a best selling book. Never mind the self esteem benefits – the contribution to your fame platform and your wallet are immense. So while Author Status is something great, Best Selling Author Status is considerably better.

Although it may seem impractical as a newbie author to contemplate such a success for your book, go ahead and contemplate. Like creating fame, there is a formula common to most non-fiction best sellers and you can replicate it to win the coveted Best Selling Author status.

There are about 100 moving parts to turning a book into a best seller and we'll look at the critical ones, but to really turn you into a believer let's look at a few realities. To start with, have you ever bought a non fiction best seller at the bookstore or airport, read the whole book and discovered that there was nothing in it? Or, more often, just a handful of useful bits of information that could have been covered in an article?

We've all bought these enticingly packaged, great-titled books only to be disappointed in the effort it took to glean the important information. It's not just you; we buy these books all the time. Take the author Suze Orman for instance. She continues to turn out best seller after best seller but her mass message was the same in the first one as in the last book: keep an eye on your credit score, spend less that you make, and before you make any financial move, stop and think to make sure it's not stupid.

This is all great advice but somehow she repackages it into book after book and they all become best sellers. At the same time you have probably read some terrific books by little known authors but they just disappear after the initial flurry around their launch. No second book, not much success with the first, and another bright spark in the non-fiction world is extinguished.

So, now that we're done bashing Suze, what's out point? It isn't the content that makes the best seller although it can help. We know the biggest-impact elements to a best seller are Publicity and Partners.

Publicity is relatively self explanatory and addressed in detail elsewhere in this book but the basic theme is you must tell people about your book; and that "telling" must be done in a strategic way. Further, although when anyone thinks publicity they envision an Oprah appearance, we believe in something more attainable.

Why not Oprah? We think an Oprah appearance will launch an author into the stratosphere as it did for Richard Carlson who wrote the Don't Sweat the Small Stuff series, Dr. Phil who writes about five pounds of books a year, and certainly Suze Orman's recent 100,000 copy-in-a-month best seller happened not coincidentally concurrent with her appearance.

However, Oprah is the Holy Grail in the publicity business and we think getting 100 other outlets, e.g., radio stations, morning television shows, city newspapers, blogs and others helping to sell your book is much more effective.

If you couple a strategic publicity plan with a partnering program, your book can really go stratospheric in an amazingly short period of time. The Chicken Soup For the Soul guys are really really good at this and have the formula down cold. The idea is that while you're doing publicity and doing personal appearances, you can leverage other people's audiences.

For instance, if your book is on Surviving and Thriving as a New Mother, traditional publicity strategy would suggest you connect with mommy bloggers to get a good review that they share with their audience. This is a great idea as far as it goes. To take it to the next level, along with geometrically increasing your book sales, you work out a revenue share deal with a mommy blogger.

How this works is simply that you offer the mommy blogger a percentage of book sales she generates, often around 15%. She might well put an advertisement/link on her website, give your book a great review and even have you on as a guest blogger or celebrity interview.

You can see how it works and this exact strategy took the Chicken Soup guys and 100 others straight to the best seller lists and straight to the bank. Who can you partner with? Bloggers, non-profits, other authors…make your list. You will be glad you did.

YOUR SECOND BOOK; ALWAYS BE WRITING

A successful book, with your name on the cover, is terrific for your personal brand and a serious fame-builder. When the final manuscript goes to the publisher it will feel like you just completed a marathon. You've earned some time off from writing and as you get busy with your book tour or the new opportunities that follow your book's release, the idea of starting your next book gets put off; for a while.

Unfortunately "a while" for most people turns into a year, then five years and a second book never happens although that time period is typically peppered with half-finished manuscripts and an indefinable feeling that you're not maximizing your professional life.

If you're serious about using fame to build a powerful personal brand remember that building and living the life that fame can give you requires constant forward movement. Please accept that you need to plan for a book a year. Look around and you'll see the biggest long term brand authors are doing this – at least until they finesse sometimes into early retirement because they have achieved their professional and financial goals.

Sometimes it seems that much of what we do for our clients involves psychology. It's easy for us to tell someone to write their next book and give them a deadline. The practicalities in most situations require something different. Only a select few people have the willpower to start their second book the day after they turn in the final manuscript on the first one.

Our recommendation for your personal writing plan is a two step process. First, while you're writing the first book, have an extra pad that is always right next to you while you write. As random thoughts occur to you, which they will, for a title and subject for your next book, write them down. As chapter subjects occur to you, write them below the relevant chapter title.

Then, once a week organize this pad into one document. The organization process will let you eliminate things that don't work and bring to the forefront some home run ideas. What you're really doing is starting your next book. If you do this from the start of your writing process, you'll always have a book in process so when book number one is complete, book number two is outlined. Thus you avoid the difficult blank page syndrome for all future books.

The final challenge faced by authors is finding the time to write. It's a cruel reality that the people with the most interesting things going on in their lives, and therefore lots to write about, are the busiest. John Grisham, one of the best selling authors of all time, gives us some good advice here. According to John, the way to become an author is to write a page a day, no matter what. If you're not doing that, you're not an author.

YOU DOT COM
YOUR POWERFUL ONLINE FOOTPRINT

"The Internet puts professional fame in the immediate reach of Everyman. It no longer takes years and a small fortune to create a nationally recognized personal brand."

—Maggie Jessup

YOU ONLINE – UNLIMITED OPPORTUNITIES FOR INTERNET FAME

Fifteen years ago it took substantial amounts of money and two or three years to launch and roll out a powerful personal brand on a national or worldwide basis. Today, principally because of technology, anyone can leverage remarkable new online tools to establish a very powerful online presence to connect with people from Singapore to Miami and Budapest.

Merge this effort with offline personal branding techniques, publicity strategies and good marketing and you've got fame. But Online is what this chapter is all about. The good news? Online personal branding is cheap and it's fast. You can have a blog in about an hour and a website by dinner time but before you head off to tell the online world you're ready for fame, you must plan strategically.

If you want to win at the fame game and build a powerful personal brand, a foundational step is creating what we call a Personal Celebrity Website. While everyone seems to accept this idea, there is often a great deal of anxiety over the very idea of creating a new site because of horror stories about expense, launch time, and design issues. There is absolutely no reason for apprehension but we completely understand where it comes from.

Way too often we have fame seekers come to us after spending twenty or even fifty thousand dollars on a website completely unnecessarily. Your personal celebrity website is nothing more, nor less, than an interactive brochure for your brand. Its purpose is to present your basic information in a compelling manner to people who are either looking at the site to "verify" that you are a person of substance, i.e., a credibility check, or to connect with you in a deeper way than is possible from merely reading your book, listening to you speak, or other single-contact activities.

For better or worse people judge you by your online presence. This works both ways of course; a one man shop in Vermont can look like a multinational conglomerate and a 200-employee industrial firm can, online, look like it has the substance of a Vermont dried flower boutique.

To build your personal brand and achieve some level of fame, your site must support the proposition that you're a member of the top one percent; the famous of your field. A well done Personal Celebrity Site will support the role you've identified for yourself. One great thing is that a nicely-done strategic celebrity site doesn't have to cost tens of thousands of dollars: you can do it on a budget; anyone can have one and every serious fame builder can have an online presence.

THE STRATEGIC CELEBRITY WEBSITE DOESN'T START WITH YOUR "TECH GUY"

Author John Grisham has a website. Martha Stewart has a website. Paris Hilton has a website. All three candidates for mayor in your home town have websites. The local gardener who gives tips on your city's television nightly news has a website. See a trend? If you want fame you must have one also. Accept this but where do you start? Probably not where you think.

Although it might seem counterintuitive, you definitely don't start with your "tech guy". Most fame seekers we meet either have a website that their tech guy did or they're planning to have this guy put one together. In both cases they feel the need to apologize either for not yet having a site or for the quality of their existing one.

They quite obviously know that it's not their best effort but they don't know how to do something better. They're frightened of the stories they've heard of $50,000 websites that take a year to get done, so they rely on their tech guy, who is someone they know and who will, for a reasonable price (cheap), create an online presence.

Note here that we aren't asking about your guy's experience. Maybe he/she has done some adequate sites for others, possibly a well known band or an up-and-coming author. To us, that doesn't matter because we are absolutely certain that one person can't create the celebrity website you need if you're looking at joining the top 1%.

Perhaps the fellow is Cisco certified a graphic artist and has been studying Flash technology for two years at the local community college. Sorry, but he's not good enough for you and here's why.

There are three elements to creating a website: graphics, content and technology. In our opinion there is no one person who is really good at graphics, content writing, and also technology. Good enough is not adequate if you really want fame. For your site to accomplish its mission you need an experienced graphics person who also understands the limitations and opportunities of web design.

You also need someone to write your content and here there is always a temptation to use your sister-in-law who teaches English or someone else with some credentials proving they've mastered the language. The person you must use for content creation is someone who can write compelling copy – effectively advertising the ultimate product: Brand You.

The third element is just as critical. Technology expertise is an important part of creating a site but it must be grounded with good business sense. In our experience everyone's guy has a need to show off all the bells and whistles he's learned over the last year. Multiple moving images (flash), podcasts, RSS feeds, data gathering, auto-populating, ecommerce and the rest.

Unfortunately, because he's learned all this functionality in the last year, none are quite perfect and they surely don't operate seamlessly or strategically. Sites end up taking too long to complete or are never completely done. There's always one more element, everyone gets frustrated at the expense and time, and you don't have the site you absolutely must have to take your steps toward fame. And at the end of the day your guy really wasn't cheap and you are not in play for the fame you want.

CELEBRITY WEBSITE PHILOSOPHY

For fame purposes you need a <u>strategic</u> personal website. It will have one single purpose: presenting and supporting Brand You. All design, layout, graphics, content, functionality and the rest should be created with that purpose in mind. While everyone faces the temptation of including every possible bit of information about themselves, avoid that lure at all costs.

What we mean by strategic when we speak of a celebrity website, at least as relates to the home page, is that a visitor will mentally qualify you in six to ten seconds as professional, interesting, seasoned, media ready, media experienced, proven and that you quite obviously fit the image/profile of a top one percent person. If you miss out on any of these items you will miss many opportunities – most of which you'll never even know about. Reporters, producers, agents, clients, customers and others eliminate options in seconds from the look of a website; there are always a dozen other choices for them.

If you think first of your website as an online brochure for yourself, focusing on the brand you are and the brand you want to become, you'll see that brevity is a plus. Before our clients learn our fame site philosophy they'll ask something like "But what about that fourth place award I won two years ago in a writing contest? It was a really big win from an important organization."

Perhaps such a victory was a substantial personal win and you're justifiably proud of the accomplishment, but it doesn't fit a top one percent image. You didn't win; you came in fourth. It was two years ago and if you have to explain the importance of the organization granting the award it won't make good home page copy where you're trying to deliver an image of substance in six seconds. A phrase as simple as "Award Winning Essayist" is an adequate and accurate way to present the win.

The Content portions of your home page (the words) must be effectively written with the precision of an advertising copywriter. You should obsess over the precise definition of the role you're presenting to the world and then describe and support it with the fewest possible words; but no fewer. Personal brand copy writing is a tough balancing act and an art rather than a science, but the watchword is Brief.

Another philosophical consideration we have for personal celebrity websites relates to the URL or website address, e.g., yourname.com. Ideally you have your first and last name dot com as the address for your site. Somewhat less desirable is your first and last name dot net but that can still be okay. Any '.biz' or other suffixes the domain providers try to sell you are completely unnecessary although in another chapter we'll talk about the benefits of a '.org' URL for your charitable work but that's another subject.

If you elect a URL other than your own name it absolutely MUST be something everyone can instantly spell. If you have to spell it for them, it's a bad URL and you can assume a busy reporter for the LA Times, who needs an expert for a story, will not take the time to try twice. Frequently new clients will come to us with what they believe to be a terrific URL, some cute combination of their business name and some technology or knock off word. We always explain, URLs are like jokes; if you have to explain them for people to understand or even spell them, they aren't good. So, just go with your name dot com.

A final web philosophy consideration is that your celebrity site, which is just the first of several websites you'll have that we'll talk about later, should be modest in size/depth. You definitely don't want to become the content provider for your industry. Remember the site has one purpose, to present and support your brand. If it qualifies you for whatever opportunity the site visitor has in mind, that's enough. If it intrigues them sufficiently to call or email you about that opportunity, the website works and anything beyond that is clutter.

TWO CRITICAL ELEMENTS OF A HIGH-IMPACT CELEBRITY WEBSITE

While the design and content of websites will vary depending on the circumstances, there are certain common elements of a strategic website that must be included for maximum impact. There is a fame strategy purpose for each component so make your best efforts on each and every one.

Your site's header should instantly convey what the site is about and in this case that's You. For most websites the main part of the header will be simply your name. Do not use flash because search engines can't read the text and they'll miss you, plus flash can be irritating. Most people who come to your site are looking for information rather than entertainment. So unless you are getting famous in the area of digital design there is no need for clever pink penguins to graphically deliver each letter of your name while visitors wait.

Below your name on your personal site is your tag line. It should be four to nine words and no longer. Deciding on your tag line can be one of the most difficult and important efforts in the entire personal branding process. If you're an actor it can be pretty easy – your tag line is Actor but it gets more complicated if you're also a musician but still a simple Actor, Singer & Songwriter can get the job done.

The tag line gets more difficult if you're a non-profit executive, a dentist, or a wholesale florist. It must precisely "tag" you and define the role you play in this world. Everyone is unique, and that's one very cool thing about fame, you get to present the best authentic you but for all those reasons we can't give you the magic formula on developing your tag line except for this advice: do not use flowery or self promoting language here. If you use The World's Best Wholesale Florist you instantly lose credibility because we're all jaded from being promised The World's Best this or that and we're always disappointed.

The next vital element for your site's home page is the key image and with just a few exceptions, if we're talking about personal branding for fame, it's a picture of you. We see people make mistakes here all the time. The biggest challenge is for some reason people can't pick their own best picture; best picture being defined as the one that presents you in your fame role to the best possible advantage. Have a brutally honest friend or unbiased outsider assist you to select the right image.

Note that this image will be what visitors' eyes are first drawn to and it must be your best authentic self. We talk about your photo shoot elsewhere in this volume but for now consider where to get this image done. This is not a glamour shot from a mall photographer attempting to give you a fake movie star look. Nor is this an image from your friend at a portrait studio who is giving you a deal.

As you consider that people you've never met will make a decision whether or not to bless you with a new opportunity based on what they see on your home page, please think of yourself as a product for the moment. The best photographer, to get the best image of Product You, is one with a track record of catalogue shots or news shots.

They may or may not be the studio that does all the "model" shots for portfolios. Call around until you find just the right person, then visit to see some of their work. More on this later and we're sure you get the idea – don't go cheap, don't go flashy, and don't get your photo done at the mall.

Look at the personal websites of some successful big brands and you'll likely see that each has the perfect photo image, their name instantly visible, and a tag line that defines effectively who they are; at least their public Who. What's next now that you have the attention of a visitor to your website?

YOUR BLOG - BRANDING, NOT RANTING

We believe no fame website is fully effective without a strategic blog. There are volumes written on how, where, why to do a Weblog – more commonly known as a blog. It might pay to read one or more of these books because we're only going to talk about a couple of key things relating to your blog; which should be presented on the Home Page of your website rather than doing an independent blog site like those available from Word Press and others.

You need a blog for two reasons: First, when someone visits your site, the Title of the Blog itself and the subtitles of individual entries will, together with the other elements of the site, help that visitor instantly qualify and define you. Second, the content of the most recent entries can give the site visitor some insight into your message, your thinking, and whether or not you can articulate that message in an interesting manner.

The caution here is to watch out for the trap that 98% of all bloggers fall in: they believe that the world cares about the details of their lives, their thoughts, their dreams…For some reason, almost everyone who has a blog just rambles on and on about things no one cares about except themselves. That's good news for you because you can be different and someone who is checking your site will appreciate it.

We have some guidelines for you to follow when adding content to your blog, presented in no particular order of importance:

- Don't blog every day unless you are reporting on current events; no one has that interesting a life so consider that every week or once a month is ample.

- An ideal length for each entry will be from 200 to 400 words; if you're using more than that number you are likely rambling.
- Don't use the blog as a platform for complaining; no one cares that Delta Airlines charged you a $300 change fee and you'll look petty for wasting your readers' time whining about it. Famous people don't sweat the small stuff.
- Each entry should be strategically tied to your message and brand; if you're a small business consultant, each entry should be information interesting to most small businesses.

Every blog title is important; many site visitors (who ideally are potential customers, clients, voters, fans...) will scan the titles of your entries – these titles should be written with the care of advertising copy.

These are some basics to differentiate you from the other 99% of bloggers out there. Quality concise content relevant to your brand is what you're looking for; all with titles that sizzle. A great test is to have someone else review your blog with the mindset of a journalist or prospective customer and then give you feedback.

With our advice for your fame site blog, note that our counsel would be different if we were talking about a blog on a company website, or for a journalist, or if it's tied to an e-commerce platform. This strategy is solely for the personal celebrity website you create to present and support your personal brand online.

FAME SEEKER: MEET, IDENTIFY & PROFILE YOUR FANS

Whether you're an insurance executive, author or would-be rock star your trip to lasting fame involves converting people who are interested in you into fans. What we're talking about here is building a fan list and it starts with data gathering on your website; but first let's look at the value of a fan list.

Some years ago we had a client who was one of those 80's television teen idols you definitely would remember but whose star had certainly faded into obscurity. He was working two hundred person venues with no upside in sight – one step above a lounge act. However, sensing a change in the music industry and intuitively believing in the value of a list of his fans, he took action.

At every event he gave away a leather tour jacket (wholesale cost when you buy 10 about $135 each but really cool looking). Prior to the show the stage man would come out holding the jacket and tell the audience they would give it away later in the show as a raffle prize. To enter you only needed to write your name, email address, and zip code on a form in the lobby and place it in the raffle basket.

One by one, person by person, fan by fan his list was born. Who wouldn't want a cool tour jacket and who wouldn't want a list of their fans? Definitely win-win and here's where it paid off. After following this strategy on his tour and simultaneously offering free songs on his website for anyone who would simply register with their name, email address, and zip code, life changed for him.

Simultaneous with his jacket tour he was offering free music downloads on his website in return for the email and zip code information. Fans from his site were interested in his personal appearances and appearance attendees were interested in his website.

He decided he was going to take a big gamble and fund a New York show at a big venue. However, in reviewing his list of zip codes he saw there were few fans in New York but there was one huge concentration in Minneapolis and another in Australia. He passed on New York but sold out an 18,000 seat basketball arena in Minnesota and found similar success in Australia. Where did the success come from? Connecting with his fan list.

The data gathering principle applies just as much if you're an author who has developed a list of 50,000 people who have bought your books. That list gives you serious power in the publishing industry. Remember, publishers now care principally about the size of your constituency and how many books you can sell on your own. A current list of 50,000 fans who might well buy your book will get a book deal at a big publisher every time.

In the alternative, once an author has a one on one relationship with 50,000 readers, it is likely time to self publish and sell directly to your fans. Would you rather get a $.65 royalty from a publisher on 100,000 books or make $5 or more per book selling 25,000 to your list of 50,000?

We could go on with example after example, but our main point regarding building your personal brand is that fans aren't limited to big name authors or entertainers. The need for a fan list carries over to the insurance guy who has 2,000 people he stays in touch with by email, the dentist who has a 500 person opted in list… You can see how it works. So where does this all start?

Your list encompasses your celebrity website where you must have a data gathering feature which is an invitation to join your list or an exchange of something valuable, e.g., 10 Strategies for Thriving in the Music Industry, in return for a new fan's email address, zip code and perhaps name.

INTERNET GEOGRAPHY – THE CONCEPT

You remember lessons in geography from your school days: cities, states, rivers, continents and the rest. This was physical geography where everything could be identified on a map of your city, state, country or even the world. This type of map is flat and can be rolled out on a table.

On this map you can identify your own footprint; maybe it is your home on a city map or perhaps you own a small business building and that, plus your home, would be your geographic footprint. We could go on describing this concept including the Louisiana purchase and other geographic concepts but the point to understand is that this type of footprint is easily identifiable on a map.

With the world wide web a new type of geography came along where people and companies had a new kind of footprint they could establish for themselves. Your website grabs a piece of that new geography – it's your footprint on this new type of map. The site has its own address and it takes up a certain amount of space. You can care for it as you would your home or business and you can add subpages to expand your footprint.

This is where our concept of Internet Geography enters the fame strategy. For clients we believe it's necessary to have a minimum of two but possibly three or more websites to stake a claim to their piece of Internet Geography, have these sites operate synergistically, and thereby expand their footprint geometrically.

For almost everyone, when we offer this element of fame building strategy two things instantly come to their mind:

Concern #1: we're selling websites so of course we recommend you have multiple ones and

Concern #2: you either just finished your personal celebrity website and you're mentally exhausted from the effort or you're just getting started and it seems like too much to think about.

Both concerns are legitimate on their face but let's look at them to get past this potential roadblock to success with your personal brand. To address the first concern, at least for our clients, we don't sell websites – we include as many sites as great personal branding requires at no additional cost to our clients. If all someone wants is a website, we don't do it. The websites are just part of our turnkey fame package and this should be the case with any publicist you hire, if you choose to hire one.

For the second concern, that you perhaps now have a great website which puts you way ahead of most people and this should be enough, for now – welcome to the top ten percent. If all you want is to be among the more successful of your field, you can stop here. However, if you're really looking for fame – that top one percent who gets to live on the good side of the velvet ropes, you're not done.

This is a defining moment for any fame seeker and those who will achieve fame understand that a lasting personal brand is the result of constant forward motion and an expanding brand typically requires some additional websites.

INTERNET GEOGRAPHY – FAME SUPPORTING EXAMPLES

Ideally you're someone who will do what it takes to achieve the peak level of success in any field and so you're still reading. Right now and assuredly more so in the future we believe Internet Geography will be the difference between a modest footprint on the world and an immense one.

This is one area where there isn't a precise formula; the thing to capture is the concept and then see how it applies to you. Everyone can benefit right now by having additional websites capturing additional attention and finessing that attention to your personal celebrity site and vice versa. These supporting websites aren't personal in nature but rather focus on the community you serve, your professional activities, your business or all of the above. Three examples should illustrate how this works.

One of our clients owns a substantial portion of a book publisher. The publishing company, as you would expect, has a great website featuring each book and each author with data gathering, sales supporting video, and compelling offers to purchase a book. All together a nice little bit of Internet Geography, or a single website. But, there's more.

Each book could have a great sub page on the publisher's site, and we do use some cool search engine strategies to make effective landing pages for each title but rather, we used the principle of Internet Geography to create independent websites for each book and author rather than the typical sub pages.

So now, when someone searches for the publisher, any title, or any author, they don't simply find just one search engine result. Instead, the publisher site comes up as does the book's independent website and several sub pages of each. Of course you know what's next – each of these is in turn linked to each author's personal celebrity website. Search engines also give each site extra points for having both outbound links as well as for inbound links. Internet Geography creates quite a footprint for the authors, the books, and the publisher.

A beautiful thing about this concept is it's like the universe – it's constantly expanding and evolving. So to continue the example let's consider that one of the authors has a company that sells dried flowers. Of course their personal celebrity site, which gives an overview of their activities, has a link to the dried flower business, but remembering that Internet Geography helps along every other fame element the dried flower business owner takes the next step.

Enter the American Association of Dried Flower Retailers and Wholesalers. One way to capture the top position in your industry is to create an association for your industry. It might start with just a hot-looking web presence with you at the head of the association but note as we're talking about web presence, this dried flower fame pro just picked up more Internet Geography.

The association site can offer the author's book, feature the author's individual business and invite others in the industry to share successful dried flower business strategies which in turn can become a booklet offered by the association, which has its own micro site…all creating a big online footprint.

This all might seem like an extreme example for a publisher, an author, a dried flower person, an association head, until you realize that the publisher also has an interest in the dried flower company and he just created a piece of Internet Geography the size of Ohio; all operating synergistically.

You might not sell books or dried flowers but you're going to be an author if you follow our counsel; you have some income producing activity and you can create an association in any industry. So, we're talking about you and the piece of Internet Geography you create for yourself. Take an hour and consider how all this might work for you; does it still seem crazy to have two, three or five websites all channeling visibility and opportunity to Brand You?

TWO MORE CELEBRITY WEBSITE ELEMENTS

No matter your profession or role, your website needs two additional elements in addition to those already covered here. A Media Room and Contact information.

Fame requires media support and endorsement, period. There is no way around this fact and you'll notice significant portions of this book address how to gather, maintain, and monetize media interest in your personal brand. It follows then that you should make yourself and your website as well presented and convenient as possible. This starts in your Media Room.

Accept the premise that if a reporter needs an expert for a piece with a five o'clock deadline and two equally competent experts are visible, the expert who makes the reporter's job easy will be the one who gets the ink. One is left by the phone not understanding why no one ever called back while the other gets 37 column inches including a flattering photograph and a high-resolution image of their new book's cover.

Your Media Room is a very visible tab on the home page of your personal celebrity site. This key element provides anyone in the media with exactly what they need to present a great article either on you or referencing you as an expert. Your Media Room will have a copy of your Media Kit and it is also a good idea to include several up-to-date photos that a reporter can take off your site to use in their story.

Also the Media Room on you dot com will include press releases, a list of article ideas that not coincidentally can be wrapped around your expertise, a list of keywords and keyphrases that describe your expertise, and an Image Gallery. The Image Gallery includes three to ten photo images of you in your various roles, e.g., author, speaker, professional person, for easy download enabling a reporter on deadline to still include a flattering image of you in the article.

The next element for your celebrity website is the contact information. While this seems obvious, many people and businesses somehow lose the critical concept that if a site visitor with an opportunity for you can't connect with you, all the other elements are wasted. There should be at least two Contact links on the home page as well as a tab that links to a contact sub page.

It will be your call whether you want to hear from people by phone or email. That depends on the nature of the fame you're looking for. A real estate person would logically want people to be able to call before they call someone else. On the other hand, an entertainer with at least a modest fan base doesn't need two, ten or fifty thousand people having her phone number. Quite literally it's your call here.

While we're on the subject of Contact information on your site, we need to look at both your email and phone numbers. It costs perhaps $20 per month to have branded email accounts and you must take this step. When you receive an email from john@johnsmith.com, does John not seem more professional than if he had connected as john@hotmail.com?. Are you going to pay Hotmail John five or ten thousand dollars to keynote at your event?

If you're an actor, you must have a Southern California phone number. Certainly agents, producers and casting people would prefer to deal with someone local, but as with many fame elements, this doesn't apply only to Hollywood. If you're looking for fame in the financial arena, it wouldn't hurt to have a New York number and a political consultant really should have a Washington DC prefix.

The concept with the "local" phone number is to make it more comfortable for someone who has an opportunity for you to call. Several Internet based phone companies like Vonage will give you a local or 'virtual' phone number in any U.S. city and many foreign countries. Many cell phone carriers will do the same. Want to look approachable, local, and substantial online? Have two or more "strategically" local phone numbers on your site's Contact information.

CREATE A POWERFUL PRESENCE

ROLE, IMAGE & MESSAGE

. . . .

"The celebrity look can be created; the sound of intelligence can be learned. Do these two things and you have the packaging for a powerful personal brand."

—Jay Jessup

. . . .

PRESENCE – WHAT IS IT?

When Al Pacino walks into a room there's a sense of power about him that is much more than what we know of him from his award winning films or the fact he's a Hollywood celebrity. Even if we had never heard of this iconic actor, he'd still radiate that commanding presence; it's the very foundation of the phenomenally successful career he's built. The same is true of Ellen DeGeneres, Sarah Palin, Steven Spielberg and even Al Gore.

If a charismatic candidate enters a room, everyone immediately senses something powerful about him or her – this is presence. At any party or business event there are always one or two people who really stand out; their self assured competence radiates a sort of aura – this is presence.

The famous in every field have developed the qualities that, when perceived together, make up that fascinating personal characteristic we define as presence. Hollywood stars have it, winning candidates have it, sports legends have it, and the Leading Voices of your own industry have this thing called presence.

If you're going to build a powerful personal brand you'll need to understand presence in detail and then learn to create it for yourself. Don't worry; almost anyone can create it and we'll show you exactly how to do it. So what is presence? Like fame itself it's something better described than defined:

- It's an extraordinary quality; it makes someone a breed apart.
- It gives people power; the type given to you by others.
- Presence doesn't intimidate; rather, it draws people in with the attitude, look, and vocals you project.
- It's a commanding distinctive projection; it's unique to you and really can't be copied although it can be learned.

- It's that combination of self-assuredness, composure, style and competence that simply radiates from someone with a powerful personal brand.

Presence is an unbeatable advantage in any competition for jobs, roles, even in sports and certainly in every arena where earning money or winning a position are measures of success. It makes people like you and want to be part of your world.

You can, should and must have the Presence advantage if you're developing a powerful brand for yourself. As with the big picture of fame, there's a formula with several elements for developing this special quality. This formula is different for every person but the essentials are: Defining your role, having the look to support that role, developing the sound of intelligence, and continuous improvement of your message.

When someone has presence you know it the moment they walk into a room; actually that's almost the test of presence – Do people immediately perceive you have this quality? You can be the one who stands out from the crowd; you can look, sound, feel and be a powerful brand with a competitive advantage. The presence development process begins by defining your role, your stage and your audience.

DEFINE YOUR ROLE, YOUR STAGE & YOUR AUDIENCE

The statement "All the world's a stage" launches the well-known monologue in William Shakespeare's *As You Like It* and we agree; you too should concur if you want to build the big kind of fame we're offering in Fame 101. Professional fame is a lot like entertainment – there is, or should be, an element of show business in every personal branding effort and you should think of yourself as always on stage.

In the fame business, the winners are entertainers; the big time lawyer, the television baker, the front page journalist and even the celebrity undertaker. We all like to be entertained, even at a funeral, and we gravitate toward people who amuse us or capture our interest; this is a fundamental of creating presence and an important element of fame.

Ideally you're trusting us for the moment and picturing yourself as an entertainer; your next question might be how do you become a successful one – a powerful personal brand? The answer is to first realize that your professional (and often personal) life is a story and that you have a role in this story. So the real question to ask yourself is What's my story and What's my role?

Your story should give you something to work with and you should make sure there's room for you to present an interesting character. Then, exactly like an actor, you prepare to play the role. It's why we believe the best pre-law students are studying drama and speech in addition to political science; it's why media trainers are so in-demand and it is exactly why the best communicators rise to the top of their profession.

We should reiterate at this point that we're not suggesting for even a moment that you become a phony; someone who isn't real. With Fame 101 you're identifying what's remarkable about yourself and then developing the best authentic you because nothing else would work. At the foundation level your role must really be your genuine self; the public loves authenticity.

However, what we are saying is that you should develop and package in the most professional manner possible all of your talents, attributes and the other things that make you unique. "Authentic" doesn't require you to skip the media training, "genuine" doesn't mean you can't get a little help from Botox or Armani, and "real" doesn't demand that you get cheap haircuts or drive bad cars.

What's really cool here is that you're the one in charge. You get every actor's dream; the chance to define your own role. At the end of the day you must do this well, then constantly work to perfect your role and play it to your advantage. Once you understand and accept the idea that Shakespeare was right, the world's a stage, you are free to develop the type of presence that is a vital part of achieving fame.

Remember, as you read Fame 101 we want you to keep asking yourself those two questions: What's my story? and What's my role? Remember also that every fame seeker needs a story because to the public and in the media it's the story that sells; not the person. Your audience must want to watch the movie, see the play or read the book before they even consider your character.

Storytellers have a special place in our society, from the Bible to the modern leaders who tell us a story of what's possible in our country and their role in making that storied image become reality. Of course you shouldn't fully define your role until you have determined your audience but that part is relatively easy if you equate "audience" with "market for your services or personal brand".

So, if you own a small business remember you're in show business; if you're launching a line of women's accessories you must have an entertaining story and if you are running for office, the winning formula always includes a bit of show biz. Define and prepare for your role, then play it with gusto.

LOOKING THE ROLE – FASHION TIPS FROM NAPOLEON & THE OLSEN TWINS

If you haven't been living in a cave for the past 20 years you know about the billion dollar phenoms Mary Kate & Ashley Olsen. They are fantastic illustrations of how to leverage the cards you're dealt, in their case a TV show when they were babies, into a cash generating professional platform.

They're masters of professional reinvention; every five years or so these twin television and film actors launch an age-appropriate acting vehicle surrounded by magazines, makeup lines, newsletters, websites, DVDs, a clothing line, and other cash spin offs of their brands. You could write a book on all the things they've done right on their path from funny-looking babies to bicoastal twenty somethings, but today we're using them for just one illustrative story.

An entire generation of kids grew up watching Mary Kate & Ashley on family friendly TV and as is frequently the case with fame, their young fans wanted to be like them. They had a unique look; their clothes were fantastic. To please their own daughters, mothers across the world wanted to find the same outfits that Mary Kate & Ashley were wearing that week but you couldn't buy these clothes anywhere.

What the Olsens did, actually what their managers and image advisors did, was find cool clothes at boutiques that looked great on young women 18 to 24 but were unavailable in the tween and early teen sizes. They bought a wardrobe and took everything to an excellent tailor and had the clothes rebuilt to fit young Mary Kate and Ashley.

This isn't an inexpensive thing to do but the result differentiated the girls and put them on the covers of every magazine relevant to teens. This publicity turned into millions more fans watching their shows and buying their DVDs. When you look at it in those terms, a thousand or even ten thousand dollars in tailoring doesn't seem like an inappropriate expense. They even launched their own clothing line which was picked up by Wal Mart, keeping in mind what made their look a success and providing it to millions of girls who wanted that look.

The quick lesson for fame seekers here is that you can do miraculous things with a good tailor. The billion dollar twins, and we call them that because that's the level of revenues they've generated over the years, used this age old secret – that's right; the Olsen's were far from the first.

Did you ever wonder why some military officers, in history or in films, look more authoritative than others? The secret is in the tailoring. Most officers get their clothes off the rack at the post exchange; the ones who want to stand out make an investment of several months pay to have a private tailor use an upgraded fabric and impeccable tailoring to subtly create a better look – a building block of presence.

What can Napoleon, Teddy Roosevelt, Desert Storm commanders and Mary Kate Olsen teach you about presence? A quality tailor is a necessity and a good one can give men, women, and even tweens a competitive advantage. It's why film studios have a fleet of phenomenal tailors in their wardrobe departments and it's a secret you can use for yourself as an early step to building your own presence.

THE TERRIBLE TOO'S FOR WOMEN – HEAD OVER HEELS

Our big picture point is that one element of presence is your appearance. We aren't talking about the "I'm 20 and Oh So Perfect" sort of appearance that is necessary only if you're trying out for one of the evening post-teen or twenty-something dramas. That is simply beauty, which is something different.

Most fame seekers wonder if they must be beautiful or handsome and hot to have presence; the quick answer is that you don't have to be stunningly gorgeous – you can be quite average or even a little ugly. Danny De Vito's career is doing just fine, isn't it? Presence here is entirely about how you present yourself and it's important because physical presentation is one of the few factors people use to categorize and qualify you within the first few seconds of meeting. It's initially about first impressions – they're all important.

As with other fame building efforts, if you want to have a strong presence you must present your best possible self and this takes strategy. Your goal should be to dress appropriately and correct for your role and for your audience, using some subtly strategic secrets to get to your own best possible look.

Volumes are written on tips for improving your look and you can spend some time doing that study later, but for now let's take a quick look at four tips for women relating to presence-killing mistakes we've seen and how you can avoid them. We'll start with what we call the Terrible Too's.

Too Much Style – Some women believe that because they spend insane amounts of money to wear the very latest styles from New York or Milan, their look just couldn't be better. Top to bottom, they're wearing the Rolls Royce of outfits and if anyone doubts how great they look they must be mistaken because these are "this year's colors" or "how slacks are worn in New York" and after all, "they're Jimmy Choos".

Unfortunately, in our experience many of the latest styles only look good if you're slightly underweight, six feet tall and no older than 19; very few of our clients or people in general fall into this physical and age category. The style rule you must follow to look great and have presence is to make wardrobe decisions based on what looks good on you; with what's in style only a secondary consideration.

Too Young or Too Old – This wardrobe trap can catch even the smartest of women and it is always deadly for presence. A simple example will make our point. If you're a fifty year old radiologist, don't shop at Forever 21. For some reason a surprising number of women believe they can take off 10 years by dressing 20 years younger; when actually the opposite is true. It may be fun but you'll never achieve the look you'll need to reach fame in your field. The people who can help you along the fame path won't take you seriously. Again, this is about appropriateness; dress just right for your age.

Too Slumped – Want to lose ten pounds and take ten years off your age? Maintain good posture; it's that simple. It turns out your mother was right. You should stand up straight, sit up straight, keep your chin up and keep your shoulders back. Bad posture is a presence-killer; you look frumpy at best but even more, you're sending out a message of personal defeat and a lack of energy. Practice good posture for just thirty days and it will become an asset for life. Take a pass on this one and you're passing on fame.

Too Bad Hair – We live in a hair-obsessed society; yours must be great or at least really good. Have you ever had someone look at your new cut or style and say "Ouch, that's too bad"? Likely not, because even your best friend will lie to you about this important presence-builder. So what can you do to get that great look? To start with, you can follow a few simple rules.

Never ever do a home perm, under no circumstances let your best friend dye your hair, if you have the same cut you did in high school it's wrong, and work nights at the local Dairy Queen if you have to so that you can afford a quality cut, style and color. Note in this area you should also watch out for the Too Much Style trap; something right for New York can make you look foolish in the rest of the world; your cut must be both great and appropriate.

A final Don't Do This for women relates to wearing heels. Sure you look taller and your butt appears to sag less in direct proportion to the height of the heel but if you don't have a thousand hours into wearing these shoes, don't wear them anywhere that matters. Nothing, except really bad hair, is more of a fame killer than a woman who wobbles or clumps in heels. How do you know when you're ready to wear heels in prime time? If you're sure you could play football or run across a cobblestone courtyard without faltering, you've earned the right to this fashion item. Practice on your own time, not in prime time.

THE CELEBRITY LOOK – IN EVERY FIELD

You will notice we focus on the word "appropriate" in deciding how to dress and look for fame. On its most basic level this means don't make any of the fashion or appearance disaster mistakes; this will at least keep you from losing your audience at that all important first impression time. However, appropriate is more than just Don't Wear Horizontal Stripes if You're Big sort of rule; rather what we mean by appropriate is Correct for your role and audience.

Once you decide what look or looks are appropriate for the role you're living, the next and critical step is to make sure you look just a little bit better than your competitors and your audience. That is the test for appropriate. This doesn't mean you should wear an Armani suit to a pool party; that's overkill and absolutely inappropriate. On the other hand if you're a man going to an event where most will be wearing business suits, the correct Armani will make you stand out.

While we're on the subject of putting together your wardrobe for fame, and as it might sound like we're pimping for Armani (although this and some other designers can make a stout man look presidential and a semi-obese woman appear elegant) remember you're not buying the label. You must buy what makes you look good.

If you're among the 99% of people who can't afford outfits that run a thousand dollars or more, you can however join the many of us who wear those clothes without spending that much. The theme here is to always buy quality but never pay retail. You can accomplish this by shopping sales at the better stores; end of the season is best and buy timeless style nine months in advance. Buying a heavy wool suit at an April sale can save 75% or more.

Another, and lesser known trick of those who dress incredibly well on a budget, is to shop at the very high end consignment stores. If you're within driving distance of upscale locales like Scottsdale, West Los Angeles, New York City, San Francisco or Palm Beach, one can find quite a few places where you can pick up a St. John outfit for five to seven hundred dollars and some barely worn Manolos at a small fraction of retail.

If you're a man and shopping at the Men's Warehouse, that isn't a stop on the path to fame. Don't go there. Are we clothes snobs? Isn't it a bit superficial to dress in high end clothes? Is an appropriate wardrobe really that important in building your fame platform? Isn't the authentic you a jeans and tee shirt?

You can find the answer for yourself. Male fame seekers, have you ever put on an Armani jacket or even a Hickey Freeman suit? Go to Nordstrom and try on several lesser brands and then slip on one of these high end items. You can instantly feel the difference; these slide on and wrap you in luxury. They make you feel special and no matter how much of a back-to-basics person you may be, you will present yourself with more confidence and authority in any group when you're wearing an appropriate, high end jacket.

Remember you're dressing for your role so unless your brand is beekeeper or you're raising a crop of granola, head for the Saks Fifth Avenue Outlet or the designer shop at Nordstrom at their end of season sale and spend what's needed to dress for the role of your lifetime.

Our female clients typically don't need to be convinced of the value of great clothing; most have already learned that a couple of flattering outfits trump a dozen average-looking ensembles. The thing you must remember though, and excuse us for the constant repetition, is to dress appropriately and only in what looks good on brand you. We went shopping for a teen client and found a Benetton brown tweed blazer – Retail $350, end of the season $50. We paired that with a pair of khakis from Gap, on sale, $20, added a T-shirt from Nordy's, and some medium heels from DSW on the clearance rack. She looked great on her appearance on Fox & Friends. Total cost of this age appropriate outfit: $125.

We could go on and on about achieving the celebrity look but there are many more subjects to cover. Just remember timeless style and dressing a little better than your audience and your peers is the formula you should follow. Back this up with a strong effort at being fit and healthy (there are 10,000 books on this subject); you'll have the look you need to achieve your maximum presence – a make-it or break-it element of fame.

SOUNDING YOUR ROLE – INTELLIGENCE, CONFIDENCE & AUTHORITY

Have you ever met someone who looked like the very picture of success: the right clothes, the right story, an appropriate stage and then they opened their mouth - and it was trailer park all the way? Usually there's a red flag early on; wrong hair, no story or maybe the wrong setting but some people get really pretty far along the path to fame with a fantastic look. Unfortunately, they ultimately hit a brick wall and fame eludes them.

Some television or commercial actors fit this model; they look like everyone's dream person but when they're unscripted they come off as seriously dumb or at a minimum inarticulate. They've been in Los Angeles long enough to learn how to get the look and fake the fame but their communication skills fail them sufficiently to doom them to a no-fame life.

And herein lies the great tragedy; we've known some beautiful, or at least beautifully packaged people, who aren't good communicators but we know for a fact that they're among the brightest people we've ever met. We've seen corporate executives who should have the world by the tail but they mumble their way to mediocrity; or a startup team with a world-changing idea but an inability to articulate their miracle.

Many such bright people are bad communicators and they have no chance at fame because of this failing. However, for you there's great news. Almost anyone can become a sparkling communication star. You can actually develop the verbal and non verbal skills needed for fame; they are learned attributes and as with every other element of building your powerful personal brand, you can become fabulously skilled with practice.

You've met the people, typically at the top of their game and their field, who can make impromptu remarks that are inspiring and memorable. Their speeches are seemingly unscripted; they speak from the heart. When you ask these stars almost any question they deliver just the right answer in an articulate manner and they're concise. They're likeable, confident and they speak with authority.

If you've read this far in Fame 101 you're likely open to the idea that everything you do can be refined and improved upon. This is absolutely true with communication skills and it's why all of our clients, even those with Obama-like presentation, go through media training, work on continuous message development and practice, practice and practice even more.

Here's the point and here's the goal: The elite of every field are fantastic communicators in every setting; whether speaking one on one or on national television. They come off as likeable ordinary people; and yet their message is memorable. They never sound rehearsed and they always seem interested, engaged and like they're pleased to be exactly where they are – former President Clinton has this skill and you can and must learn it too.

To build and maximize your platform for a powerful personal brand you must develop this authority, confidence and off-the-cuff likeability that quality communication delivers. Remembering that no matter how good a communicator you are, you can always be better - let's look at how to take you from good to great.

THE SOUND OF INTELLIGENCE – HERE'S HOW TO GET IT

Why one person reaches the peak of fame while another doesn't is somewhat complex, but one thing is clear: great messaging is a necessary part of the ticket to membership in this elite group. Very simply, successful people have the sound of intelligence and the messaging to back it up. Both are skills that you can learn and how successful you become will be directly tied to your ability to deliver on these two concepts.

Let's consider first this "sound" you need. Go online and listen to some great speeches by Winston Churchill or Martin Luther King Jr. as well as some good presentations from leaders in your own or really any field. Listen to them but focus not on what they're saying but rather on how they are saying it. What you're looking to identify is the phonetic sound; it's the sound of sophistication and the sound of knowing what they're talking about.

Communicators with the sound of intelligence aren't rambling, ever. They don't say "Um" and they don't say "Uh". Their cadence is perfect; it's been refined and practiced to a level where it doesn't sound practiced. Their sound is never arrogant; they don't talk down. Their likeablility quotient is very high. They weave in the correct industry jargon, the words and phrases from that field, but not too much – they know the art of creating the perfect balance.

Beyond their rhythm, pace and intonation, great communicators always weave in a bit of drama – certainly in their speeches. You might believe that drama can't be found in a technical subject or for a PTA speech but it certainly can. Your medical device can be described as an "important step forward for the health of mankind", the new fourth grade reading books are "a building block in the education foundation for the future leaders of our country" and little Sally's lemonade stand really "represents a microcosm of the entrepreneurial DNA upon which our great country was built".

While these are off-the-wall examples, each illustrates our point that memorable communication makes a connection with something emotional – a snippet of speech that makes you snap your head around when you hear it. To capture the sound of intelligence, you must weave in just a small bit of the dramatic into your communication.

The end game here is for your audience, whether one person or one thousand or a mass of television viewers, to think to themselves "Hey, she really knows what she's talking about." With the sound of intelligence, you can make this happen. In our experience it isn't the audience's understanding of your message but a feeling they get when a speaker delivers with this sound of intelligence.

To clear the path to become a top one percenter in your field, we've told you that you must have both this sound we talk about as well as the knowledge and messaging to communicate in the best manner possible. Let's now look at the second part of this equation – your message.

YOUR MESSAGE CONTENT

We are constantly astounded by the amazing tools and models taught in America's schools and colleges. As compared with even a dozen years ago, our country's advanced education concepts are without peer and the real-life applications can have amazing results. This is certainly true in the business field but as you'll see, some of these have applications for every professional, from actor to startup guru.

We heard an example of this just last week. A young friend attends a prestigious business school and is absolutely thriving. We always look forward to her reports of what and how she's learning but one lesson in her very first semester stands out for us as of phenomenal value.

One class is focused solely on message development and delivery. Students spend months developing two things: First, a powerful response to the question we all hear in business settings "What do you do?" and second, crafting what many of us call an "elevator pitch".

Remembering that people form their opinions of you from first impressions, you should have a lock on the ability to answer what is typically their very first question. When asked "What do you do?" have you got a great response or do you ramble or present an otherwise exciting position as something much less?

Let's look at an example. What do you do? "We have a tech company that is developing a device-agnostic platform and application for streaming HD video to your cellular appliance". Yawn; this surely doesn't create the image of a high end communicator. Perhaps people will label you as Smart but definitely not Memorable and therefore not fame-worthy.

Deliver the same information as "I'm part of a startup that helps you get the latest Gossip Girl episode in High Definition on any cell phone." Which response is more intriguing, opens a conversation, and delivers a powerful response? The reason we continue to cite tech industry examples such as this one is because some of the true innovators of our time are stalled just short of immense success because of their inability to communicate with non-tech finance people and less-tech potential customers.

So "What do you do?" from week-one at the business school and it's followed by spending time on your elevator pitch. An elevator pitch is a concise overview of your idea or concept that can be delivered in the time it takes for an elevator ride. We think the school is brilliant for spotlighting the importance of a concise message.

Crisp, concise messaging is important not only from a business communication standpoint but in the personal branding area as well; actually the two are inextricably tied together. The ability to explain a complicated subject, that has taken you perhaps years to master, so that your listener can comfortably grasp your message, is an important talent in the business world and a mandatory ability if you're looking for fame in any industry.

Actors, business people, scientists, authors, non profit heads and everyone else should have a rock solid elevator pitch that they've refined and refined again. Of course as you remember from earlier in the chapter you need to be able to deliver the pitch in a seemingly unpracticed manner; as if it's the first time you've ever said it in precisely this manner and that you're completely excited about the message.

We could go on, as does the business school's curriculum we referenced above, with looking at your Big Speech and looking at the value of a voice coach, presentation development and training, or other key communication concepts but there are a thousand resources for that information.

Our point in this section is that you can and must become a great communicator in order to build the powerful personal brand that is part of fame. Ideally you now see the distinction between the artificial-sounding media bytes delivered by losing politicians and the ability to immediately convey authority, confidence and power. Steven Jobs, Donald Trump, Suze Orman, Martha Stewart and the elite of your industry can do this – you can too.

FAME FUEL
MEDIA EXPOSURE
AND HOW TO GET IT

. . . .

"On most days there just isn't that much breaking news but the networks as well as radio, print and online outlets still must fill minutes, column inches, and on-air hours with content. If you are mediagenic and have something to offer, the media will enthusiastically welcome you." —Maggie Jessup

. . . .

"I SAW YOU ON GOOD MORNING AMERICA!"

Is there any possibility that Paula Deen would have a hot television show, a massively successful magazine, multiple book deals, an impossible-to-get-in restaurant and an amazing income without media exposure? Zero possibility. Precisely overnight, a USA Today article and a Home Shopping Network appearance launched this fifty-something unknown personal brand to American icon status.

If fame is the most powerful force in the universe, publicity is the fuel that feeds and maintains that power for people who know the rules and realities of getting media exposure. Paula used the media to catapult herself onto the national stage. The lesson here is that you can't have fame, you won't become a best selling author and you will not rise to the top of your field unless you enlist the media's help; that's done using publicity.

The reasoning behind publicity is simple: No one knows you're there until you tell them and no one knows what you do unless you tell them. Publicity tools and techniques are used to enlist the media to tell massive numbers of people who you are and what you do. When used correctly, publicity will get the media on your side which in turn will put you on the fast track to fame.

One of the most satisfying elements of our professional lives is when we're building a personal brand for a publicity novice. We get them packaged and media trained; then comes the big moment – their first big television appearance. They're thrilled and they enjoy it of course but the truly excited call always follows a day or two later when a neighbor, an old acquaintance or even a stranger stops them and says "I saw you on Good Morning America!"

Whether you're a doctor, an air traffic controller or Hollywood-series newbie, it's a fantastic feeling when people recognize you as a celebrity because your story was in the newspaper or on television. The first few times you're recognized are magical and what's even better is that this great feeling continues as more and more people recognize you in more and more places as your media exposure expands.

It's pretty great to have a U.S. Senator, a news anchor or other notable say upon meeting you "We haven't met but I have certainly heard about all the great things you're doing." We get this all the time, as do our clients, and none of us ever gets tired of it. This social/business benefit comes with membership in the fame club.

If you think, even for a moment, that you can't use publicity to get in the news; that for some reason your story isn't newsworthy – you're wrong. If you know how to do it, you can be on the radio, on television and in the magazines within a very short time period. By the time you finish reading Fame 101 you'll know exactly how to make this happen for yourself and how to make sure your story is newsworthy.

Here's something that most people don't know – very few people or companies are using publicity to achieve their goals. We can't imagine why they aren't taking action but they are missing out on the most cost effective way to promote their personal brand and their business or profession.

If you make an intelligent effort at using publicity to get media exposure, you will be miles ahead of your competition. To make you even more at ease that you'll have a strategic advantage, believe us when we say that even among those people who are using publicity, more than 80% are doing it wrong. It could even be 90%; but it won't be you because we're showing you exactly how to use publicity to get maximum media exposure.

POSITIVE MEDIA ATTENTION: BENEFITS AND MORE BENEFITS

When the Oprah Show features yet another diet, where did this story come from? Well, you now know it all started with publicity but it wasn't just a quick call to an Oprah producer to see if they want this new weight loss package on their show next week. Brand coups such as an Oprah appearance are typically the result of a year-long or even a multiple year publicity plan. Capturing media attention, with the Oprah Show being the Holy Grail, is not an easy process.

It's going to take some work, actually a lot of work. Is it worth the expense and effort? The answer is an unqualified Yes! The benefits of appearing on Oprah, and they are legion, exemplify all the reasons that publicity is great and necessary for building a powerful personal brand. As this chapter is all about the many things you must do to get press, let's first take a look at the benefits that an article about you, a television appearance, or big speech will deliver.

The advantages of media exposure parallel the benefits of fame. The only difference is that fame is the whole powerful personal brand package and publicity is one element of the "powerful" part. So exactly what are these benefits?

Credibility: Simply being on television delivers believability; it's the way our society works. We expect our news and information outlets to vet the people they present to us as experts so we're very likely to believe what those vetees have to say. While many might debate the sagacity of this view, no one would deny that when you're in the media your trustworthiness factor is enhanced. In the end, believability and trustworthiness are the elements of credibility and this is one wonderful benefit for your personal brand from media attention.

Expert Status: Nothing affirms your position as an expert, and remember America has a love affair with experts, more than regular media appearances. If the media goes to you for an opinion, you must be one of the leading voices of your field. If they do it often, you really do have Leading Voice status which is one of the defining factors of a powerful personal brand. On every newscast you'll hear something like this: "And here we have aviation expert Bob Smith to provide insight into the KLB near-miss at Heathrow Airport today. Bob, what could have been the causes of this potentially disastrous situation?" The idea is that you want to be the "Bob" of your field. The media can give you Bob's expert status almost overnight.

Geographic Brand Expansion: With enough effort, and over time, you can build a great reputation in your community by being engaged and involved. It can be done without publicity, however, the limitation here is that you're limited to the geographic area where you can personally connect with the local population. The media gives you a way to connect with people in the next town, another state or even in a country on the other side of the world. When you appear in Business Week, your personal brand is in front of readers in Miami, Omaha, and London. Great personal brands are typically national in scope, if not international. The only way to make this happen, other than social media strategy which we address elsewhere, is for the media to spread your brand to far away places.

Whether it's credibility, expert status, geographic brand expansion or a million-selling book from a single Oprah appearance, media attention is a necessary powerful brand builder as well as an absolute prerequisite to fame.

NEWS & INFORMATION

Twenty years ago, just prior to the birth of the CNN-inspired 24 hour news reporting cycle, there was a morning news hour and evening news hour; that's it. Television networks focused on breaking news, defined as what's happening now and the day's news, defined as what happened since the last newscast. That was pretty much the twice daily television news with sometimes a short cute-kid or spunky-grandmother feel-good story to close.

If you wanted to be on the news or in the news you had to have done something that very day; publicists strained to create events or announcements or even the historic "publicity stunts" to qualify as something that happened that day. Reporters were constantly on the road wanting to be on the scene for the big story, to uncover the new scandal or capture a front page photo.

Those days went away with the proliferation of news outlets. Now it's 100 channels, hundreds of magazines, blogs, and online news outlets and this list is far from exhaustive. When we put a news release on the wires these days it's not unusual for a San Francisco business story to get picked up in India and the UK.

Concurrent with the geometric expansion of news outlets, we have seen "breaking news" morph into "news" and ultimately expand into "news and information". The reason for this progression is there is nowhere near enough breaking news, or even traditional news to feed the now 50,000 journalists who are trying to fill a half million on-air minutes or column-inches daily.

All this is great news for you, the person who understands the value of media exposure and how to use it to build their brand. These 50,000 journalists are now on the hunt for information and it doesn't need to be breaking news. They want valuable and interesting stories to inform and amuse their readers or viewers.

To get media exposure you certainly monitor the daily news cycle in case you can tie your expertise to current events. An excellent strategy here is to check the New York Times online headlines each evening; the next morning editors meet to look for stories that tie in to those subjects. Was there an air crash? Are you an aviation disaster lawyer? It's time to comment. Is there a breakthrough study on the failures of public education? Are you a fame-seeking educator? It's definitely time to comment; we'll give you the tools to do that in the next section.

While commenting or providing new information or spin on breaking news is the traditional method of getting exposure, you must also follow an ongoing strategy of information distribution that will not be tied to breaking news. Of course if you're in the entertainment business it's just the daily goings on of the celebrities but in all other fields there's a way to get into the "information cycle" which has grown much much larger than the news cycle.

You can always get some press for providing information on interesting trends or anything newly-packaged about dieting, relationships or getting rich. There are a hundred other subjects that the information-vacuum we call media will pick up and distribute but the point here is that there is plenty of room for you to get the media's attention; it doesn't need to be breaking news. Let's have a look at exactly what you should and shouldn't do to get the press behind your brand building effort.

WHAT THE MEDIA WANTS – IT'S YOUR STORY, NOT YOU

We have interesting and talented people come to us all the time with the very same challenge. No matter how hard they try, they can't seem to break into the media; the local paper won't cover their activities, regional outlets seemingly couldn't care less and they believe national press is completely beyond their reach. They are truly interesting, talented professionals but something is holding them back media-wise. They want to know why they're outsiders looking in on the media environment and how to get past this rock-solid barrier to fame.

Almost universally we find these frustrated media-starved folks are breaking what we call the First Rule of getting media exposure. The rule is simple: Push your story, not yourself. If you follow that simple rule, it is a thousand percent more likely that the media will give you the coverage that you need to make it to the peak of your profession.

Here's something you might not expect; the famous and micro-niche fame folks keep their egos in check. The ability to do this is a necessary personal trait for fame and it's something that gets in the way of many, many people on their fame quest. It's surely understandable how a very intelligent and talented person can become vain, egotistical, and self-centered, especially when they get their first taste of fame but you must not fall into this trap. The most successful fame seekers and the people who have lasting fame are just not self-centered; the only narrow exception to this is if being a spoiled brat is part of their branding and how they keep themselves in the news.

The message here is directly involved with getting media exposure. You must accept that the media does not care about you; even if you're Hannah Montana, Pamela Anderson, or Joe Biden. The reason the media couldn't care less about you is that their readers and audience do not care about you, no matter who you are. This knowledge is the basis of this first rule for getting media exposure.

Your media outreach must focus on your story, not you. No one cares that you wrote a book, have a doctoral degree from Oxford, or have a new television show. However, with properly presented information, millions will care that your new book offers an effective new weight loss strategy, you've uncovered an anti-aging gene, or there's a new reality show where couples compete to win a dream wedding, matching Harleys, and a tattoo makeover.

All you need to accept, remember and act on is that publicity is not about getting your name in the newspaper or your face on television; it's about spreading your message and your brand in a way that gives the media a good story. That's all they really want, it's not asking much but they are constantly bombarded with "Look at me" personal brands rather than "Here's a cool story" people. No wonder many journalists become jaded but how great for you that media professionals so readily spread the word of a good story. So what's your story?

BRAND YOURSELF NATIONALLY BUT LOCALIZE YOUR STORY FOR MAXIMUM MEDIA

There's a trap that captures many of the could-be-famous and it's supported by countless books on publicity, but you must avoid it at all costs; the books are wrong and it's a huge barrier to fame. Here it is: the traditional thinking is that a publicity effort should begin locally. This wrong-thinking suggests you should spend a year or two or three becoming a local celebrity in your field.

Chamber of commerce networking events, local charity work, connecting with the local reporters, and getting the very occasional slot on the local news is the recommended first step by the publicity authors out there. While all of these are cool activities and you should consider them as a small part of your brand building, the power brands out there build a national brand and this is the difference between the famous and the others who get stuck in their local geographic region.

In our experience one person can only get so much local press; no matter how fascinating you are, the nightly news can only use you a couple of times a year. Your hometown newspaper editor won't permit a reporter to do more than two or three articles each year that feature you and these get harder and harder to get. If media exposure is a critical element of fame, you can see how you might get boxed in to your local community.

In contrast, if you can be part of a national story that gets picked up by the AP (Associated Press), your story may run in Austin, Indianapolis, Atlanta and Bakersfield today as well as London, Miami and Podunk tomorrow. The situation is this: if you build your brand and your story to be non-geography specific, you can pitch it to reporters across the country or even around the world.

Ideally this concept, together with other fame counsel in Fame 101, will keep you on track to build a national personal brand but this leads us to some further key advice for getting media exposure. While your brand and story may be national in scope, the story you're pitching at any given moment must have local ties. This is another golden rule of getting press.

Here's an example: the big story this year is the rocky economy. As a business consultant to universities you should have a continuous stream of commentary relating to challenges in the economy and how they relate to funding and programs for public and private colleges. Simple, yes? Actually, not.

While the strategy is correct in building your personal brand for the national stage, most of the media won't pick up your story. You may get a big appearance on a national television show or a feature in USA Today but your exposure will be one-time and you'll miss out on fifty regional media opportunities.

A reporter at the San Francisco Chronicle might find it interesting that universities are facing challenges because of the down economy but they are unlikely to do a story because it won't capture specific local interest. On the other hand, if you go to the trouble of localizing the commentary you distribute, you may well get articles and appearances all around the country.

In this case the strategy is to tie your national brand to a local university or universities; even better, tie it to real people – the students. If a nationally recognized expert, coincidentally Brand You, says that many college students from San Francisco State and UC Berkeley will lose tuition funding due to the elimination of a federal financial support program in the newly slashed budget – that's a story a Chronicle education reporter will jump on.

You'll learn elsewhere in Fame 101 the how's and why's of building a national brand for yourself but for the purposes of capturing media exposure it's this second step, localizing your national story, which can get you in the news and keep you there.

THE ART OF THE PRESS RELEASE

Press releases are the principal way you take your message to the media. Most, even those written by public relations self-called experts are inadequate, and this creates a challenge for you. When tens of thousands of releases go out weekly, with most of them being self-pitching poorly written nonsense, it's hard for your release to stand out and most get deleted or tossed out without being read. However, it is necessary for your fame build to do them so let's look at how to make yours stand out.

A press release has one purpose, although there are search engine optimization benefits discussed elsewhere in Fame 101, and that purpose is to capture the attention of someone in the media and to prompt them to call you for more information. To make this happen you will need a compelling title and tag line. We could easily write a three volume set on writing great copy for press releases but there are many resources out there and we suggest you spend some time learning this skill.

The principal theme however, is that this compelling title will be in the form of advice, solutions to common problems, an opposing opinion, create a crisis of some sort; effectively any format that presents your message as valuable to the ultimate audience and presented in an intriguing manner.

If you present a compelling title and tag line on your release you'll earn about 10 seconds of a journalist's time. Don't waste it. Your release should be concise and have just one subject. We know from personal experience in the newsroom that reporters will read no more than the release title if there are more than a few hundred words. Any subject can be reduced, for press release purposes, to three hundred and fifty words. If you can't do this, enlist the aid of a release writer.

It's really easy to keep a release short if you stick to just one subject and your chances of success skyrocket if you can manage this skill. Way too often we'll see business clients pass around a draft release with every department adding in a self-serving paragraph about their product or activities; the result is horrific. For instance, a company might have a new supplement that improves your vision.

This has huge press release potential but when one department adds that they also have products that are good for your hair, maximize your diet efforts and that their products won an industry award last week, it gets tedious. When the next department adds that a new division, headed by an industry leader recruited from a competitor, just opened, the release is terminally flawed. And yet, these are the typical releases.

Our apologies for the rant but bad press releases completely block a terrific tool to help you along the avenue to fame; yet most people turn out trash. Remember, single subject releases get press: anything else misses the boat.

You now know how to turn out a great press release but what's next? How do you get it into the right hands? Some publicity pros say you should use the several services that distribute your release to thousands of people in the media. The costs of this strategy vary from $150 per release, with a $2000 annual subscription to one of several major services, to several free press release distribution services.

To some extent you get what you pay for and we like the professional services, even with the cost but research the options and see what's right for you. So we agree that mass distribution of your release is good; however, we think that's only a part of the right strategy.

To get press, you need to cast a wide net with your release distribution but you also need a targeted effort. Thus you should also build a targeted list, or have your publicity firm do it for you, of reporters, bloggers, and producers who cover your subject that are geographically relevant. This list can be anywhere from 20 to 120 media people who are most likely to be interested in your message. You should stay in touch with them regularly to get them accustomed to seeing your name and each contact with a release should be personalized.

It's this personalization that will get your release noticed over hundreds of others they see from the mass distribution services. Consider this example: "Dear Katie, Your article about the three teachers who are rolling out a new foreign language immersion pilot program was fascinating. I thought you might have an interest in a total-immersion technology course we put together here at Will Rogers Middle School. Immersion learning hits a whole new level of effectiveness and I'd love to talk to you about it sometime. I've attached a release; if you'd like more information give me a call".

The media needs stories and they will give you all the coverage you can handle if you follow these simple press release rules to get your information in their hands. A short and concise release with a compelling title, personally targeted where possible, is how you harness the power of the press release to build your personal brand.

THERE'S NO OSCAR FOR BEST PUBLICIST

While this chapter has taught you how to use publicity to leverage your brand message in some terrific ways, we would be remiss if we didn't follow up with an additional bit of advice. You should remember that when the media puts you in the national spotlight, it was because they "discovered" your story. Sure you know that your publicist beat down their door for a year to get their interest but that is irrelevant and should never be shared with your audience. It's okay to have a publicist, certainly it's recommended from our standpoint but when someone asks how you made People Magazine, it's best to respond with a shrug and say "They just called me." Let's look at some examples.

When John Travolta walks on Ellen's stage, does a photo shoot for the cover of Vanity Fair or gives his acceptance speech at the Academy Awards, he doesn't thank his publicist. As a matter of fact, have you ever heard anyone with any kind of fame thank or even acknowledge the behind-the-scenes publicity guru who got them the gig?

The president of your company was selected to keynote at the charity dinner because of publicity and the parent of a child at your son's school got a great book deal principally because of their publicist. Certainly the president had to be a good speaker and the parent's book had to be good but there are many potential keynotes and a hundred thousand children's books looking for a publisher. Speaking engagements, book deals and other of life's greatest fruits come from media exposure and that all happens because of your publicist.

Publicists get you media coverage and with the exception of only the very biggest entertainment industry superstars, it's the publicist who gets the tech star the cover of Fast Company magazine, gets the naturopath a weekly spot on local television and puts your district's best teacher in contention for a national Teacher of the Year award. And yet, no public thank you's – ever. What's up with that?

If a publicist does their job right, your media exposure apparently comes from journalists "discovering" your story and including it in their daily column or television news show. The media found you out and found you fascinating. This plays on the public perception of reporters as society's Jimmy Olsens who are constantly out on the streets looking for the next big story.

In reality, reduced news staffs have more or less shackled reporters to their offices and the vast majority of stories are brought to their attention by a publicist; the interview follows. So there are two points here: no matter how interesting your story, the media is unlikely to come to you and once you do get the media attention, the role of the publicist should stay private.

It kills the whole fame image if your constituents consider that the article in US Magazine was the result of a publicist calling acquaintances at twenty different A List publications to pitch your story and the US Magazine editor was the one who saw the fit. Thus, you never bring up the role of your publicist; fame insiders all know how it works but most people simply have no idea.

For fame, you'll need the media exposure and publicity will get it for you, but the scores of articles and dozens of television appearances must be perceived as coming from an uninvited inquiry from the press. The media found your story and followed up; the ensuing national recognition was simply a logical progression.

Nothing here is meant to discount the value or appeal of your story. The thing that makes you remarkable really is valuable information and the public will very likely be interested in your personal brand. It's simply that publicists, using publicity, are the vehicle to getting media attention in the first place.

Should you thank your publicist for making this all happen? Certainly yes, but privately. Insofar as everyone else is concerned, you're as amazed as anyone at how the media picked up on your story, it spread across the nation and seems to keep going on its own.

So, no matter how tempted you are to brag about your cool new publicist, and these days it does have a certain coolness factor, don't do it. Talking about your publicist dilutes the value of the media exposure you do get and to join the ranks of the famous, you need all the press you can get.

SUCCESSFUL PERSONAL BRANDS

SKIP THE ROOKIE MEDIA BLUNDERS

"In any society fame is the most powerful thing; it's the very thing that defines social order."

—Jay Jessup

MEDIA MISTAKES AND HOW TO AVOID THEM

No one knows you're there until you tell them is the foundational explanation of the need for publicity and every big personal brand understands the value of using publicity to garner media attention. Simple, yes? Absolutely, as far as the statement goes. What we must address however are some common pitfalls that fame-savvy people have learned to avoid when dealing with reporters, bloggers, producers, and the other key media players.

These are the very people who can loan you a national stage and cause your career to jump forward a decade in a matter of months. We cannot overstate the importance of your relationship with this power center, collectively called *The Media*. They can give fame or they can take it away.

Most people have never had any meaningful contact with a local reporter, much less a regional news anchor, morning show producer, even less with anyone on the team that produces national television or a major magazine. Thus, it is understandable when mistakes are made.

Many of you started reading this book with the idea that public relations or publicity was basically a press release and a phone call from your publicist that was the combination that put you on Good Morning America. While the release and the publicist – producer connection are certainly key in this effort, those are just the enabling efforts. The real substance of the effort is up to you.

Most of this volume teaches you to build fame infrastructure around your role and your message and then to roll out the final packaged product using the media and other resources for leverage. The thing that can go terribly wrong or magnificently right is how you handle the media.

We are assuming most of you are media rookies and likely to fall into the invisible traps surrounding the path to becoming what some reference as a media darling of your field. As we have been building and managing personal brands for quite a few years we have seen many of these traps and learned how to avoid them. This chapter is to help you skip your rookie year as relates to working with the media.

What follows are the typical mistakes, all of which you will encounter in the course of your newly amazing fame-supported career. If you can simply keep them in mind you won't find yourself derailed by any of these sometimes career-killing errors.

No matter how unlikely some may seem, we have seen every one of these scenarios played out multiple times. What is so tragic is that some blunders, because of their very public nature, can overturn a skyrocketing personal brand in a minute or less. They have left presidential hopefuls, near titan-level business stars, and undoubtedly several high potential people from your own industry in branding Hell alongside the fame path watching their competitors travel past.

Truly this chapter is not meant to scare you. In fact the cautions are quite simple to follow; we merely want you to understand the severity of the consequences if you develop a cavalier attitude toward the media. Remember: if you do this right, meaning a well-founded smart publicity program, you have a trip to your career dreams in store.

SMART PERSONAL BRANDS KNOW THEY ARE ALWAYS ON THE RECORD

Pitfall number one is the potentially dangerous phrase "off the record". Many careers have been shattered, countless deep personal secrets have been exposed, and too many fame seeking newbies have been derailed by relying on this concept. The idea is simple, when you're talking to a member of the media, you both know that whatever you say is fair game to use in an article or as a basis for further investigation into their story. That's because the interview or conversation is "on the record."

The challenge is that sometimes, to be helpful or to provide further explanation of what you're saying, you want to convey some information that you received in confidence or perhaps do not want to see in print. Here is where you learn about "off the record" as well as the integrity of the media person. One would think journalistic integrity would require that anything you say under this protective phrase will never be seen in print.

Although the majority of reporters will honor the deal once they've agreed the information is given as background rather than for the record, some do not. And, it's because of these media miscreants that the smart thing to do is to always assume anything you say is on the record. The only exception to this might be when you have a longstanding relationship with a reporter but even then, it is much better to err on the side of caution.

By way of example if a reporter asks "Off the record, what do you Really think of the new vice president?" You might think the vp is a moron with the ethics of a junk yard dog but unless you want to see it in print, keep it to yourself. Avoid the temptation and settle for a non-answer such as "He's a very special guy." This illustration is obvious but the same thought process carries over to revealing a source in an "Off the record, where did you hear that?" or a hundred other potentially damaging scenarios.

We might as well warn you about two techniques, along these same lines, in a reporter's bag of tricks you will need to watch out for as you get more and more visible. First, in the typical interview the reporter is furiously scribbling notes and it's all very intense. Toward the end however, they sometimes visibly relax and put the pen down. You might think the interview is over and offer a too-casual response to "What a great interview. Do you REALLY think the vice president is a sharp fellow? Come on, what do you think?"

Just because the pen is down doesn't mean you're off the record. No doubt you can see the potentially calamitous results of this publicity faux pas. The cautions are also in order for on-camera interviews. Watch the green/red light. Just because the interview is seemingly "over" doesn't mean you're not still on camera. President Reagan learned this with a flippant remark about nuking America's biggest enemy post-interview but still on camera. It was the lead story across our country… and across Theirs!

WHEN HOLDING BACK IS AN INTERVIEW KILLER

A year or two ago we watched an author completely bomb during a national television interview. It was painful for us as viewers, so painful for the interviewer that she actually walked off the stage, and a death blow to the author who turned a potentially career making opportunity into a crushing defeat. This all happened in about two minutes; such is the power and reach of the media. For the record, she wasn't one of our clients.

So here's the story. A major news celebrity was interviewing an author about her new book. This happens all the time and these are usually the easiest sort of media opportunities because the interviewer will tee you up, time after time, to make yourself look good and the book look desirable. Easy questions designed for informative home run answers. What can go wrong here?

Something definitely went awry because the author had apparently gotten some truly bad advice. We believe she bought one of these Get On Oprah Overnight sort of books that tells an author that one way to sell more books is to be coy during interviews so viewers will want to rush out and learn more.

This is really bad counsel to start with but the author took it to the extreme. When the interviewer, again one of the top three most notable in the United States, asked her first question, the author gave a several word response and said "Well that's all covered in my book." You can likely see the rest coming, can't you?

Question two was something as simple as "What are a few of the things...."; the author's response: "That's all covered in my book." The always professional interviewer took this in stride and asked yet another question about the book's content and how a reader might benefit. Again, the same several word response followed by "When they buy my book they'll learn all about that."

It is really tough to get a big national brand media host to lose their cool; suffering and supporting fools is something they accept as part of their job. However, the author managed to push this interviewer's outrage button. On set, on camera, during the live show the questioner stood up and quite clearly told the author that her purpose was to get great information for her audience, not to sell the author's book. She walked off stage, leaving the author confused as to what she had done wrong, and then the show broke for a commercial. Word got around and the author's tour was cancelled.

Our message here is, and it's the secret to getting return invitations to television and radio shows, always share as much valuable information as you can during the interview. Readily give away 60% or more of the content of your book or the service you sell. The thing to remember is that you're not selling the formula for Big Mac sauce or original Coca Cola; your product is much broader than that and is not super secret or you wouldn't have written the book.

People buy books most often because of some exposure to the author. If they like the author and are intrigued by what they hear or read, they buy the book. The way to intrigue people is to share as much of your very best content as you can. The second point is that in the case of the exiting media interviewer, she was absolutely correct in saying that these shows are to inform (and entertain) the audience. Show producers share their audience with people who can do just that; amuse and intrigue the viewers. There is an implied agreement that if you're on the show you'll do your very best to contribute to this effort.

You probably don't need any more examples to understand the message of this section. The now media-shunned author made a rookie mistake that a well-prepared powerful personal brand would never allow to happen. When you're doing interviews, share all of your best information. The audience will benefit and so will you with book sales and return invitations.

LEADING VOICES OFFER SHOWS RATHER THAN PERSONAL PROMOTION

A surprising number of people believe they are so fascinating that Oprah or Ellen or the rest could easily do an entire show just on them; maybe even two shows with one covering their book and the other their professional activities and plans. And so, when they pitch themselves to the media or find a publicist to pursue this flawed strategy, their presentation is all about them, not the audience.

Every television producer, editor or reporter has just one thing in mind: how to create a program that their audience will love. They make their decisions based on which people and stories are available to them at any given time. And so, unless you are one of the perhaps 10 iconic figures of our time, accept ahead of time that an entire show about you just isn't going to happen; at least not on major media.

So, what's the idea here? There is a successful pitch strategy that we learned from an author who launched on Oprah. He had a phenomenal writing career from that moment on with sometimes more than one book on the NY Times best seller list at the same time. His explanation for this ongoing phenomenon started with the Oprah launch but was kept going by his tremendous talent for getting himself consistently booked on great television and radio shows.

We were obviously sitting on the edge of our chairs as he shared his secret with us over lunch at his home. His easy strategy, and one we have followed to this day, is prior to connecting with a producer he would think of one or more great shows he would love to watch as a typical audience member that would include him as part of the production.

When he had thought of a terrific panel, into which his work would fit, he would think through the show and then, and only then, get ready to pitch. Simple, brilliant, and effective. If you doubt this, put yourself in a producer's position. Caller number one tells you about a book he has on relationships and explains why he is an expert. This is traditional publicity.

The more evolved pitch person, following our friend's presentation advice, would suggest a pre-Valentines Day show on relationships, including as guests the owner of a successful online dating site, a relationship columnist from one of the major newspapers, and for example, our friend who is a psychologist with a sub specialty of counseling patients in this specific area and coincidentally the author of a new book on the subject.

You, the producer, are going to like the second caller much better because he is focused on helping you solve your ongoing problem – how to fill on-air time with consistently great programming. Yours can be a much better offer than the customary self-pitch. So before you start to connect with the media, come up with some terrific story ideas that include your product or services as key elements of a larger story.

Some very successful personal brands even include a list of story ideas in the Media Room section of their website. Try the story-pitch plan for a few months and we are certain you will marvel at how frequently you find yourself on camera because the media embraced your helpful approach.

WIN MEDIA COVERAGE BY AVOIDING THE
ADVERTISER MINDSET

A big branding success driver is your excitement about the products and services you have to offer and the benefits they will bring to your target markets. Enthusiasm is terrific and when it shows through in a sales situation or a media interview, the odds of your success are immeasurably enhanced.

The big *however* is that you must avoid one pitfall that entraps perhaps ninety percent of all people and companies that are seeking media attention. Their underlying failure is that they do not understand the distinction between publicity and advertising or if they do see the difference they are so overcome with the value of their services or products that they fail to remember this trap when connecting with bloggers, reporters, and other media insiders.

The thing to bear in mind is the more you remind a reporter that your contact is commercially motivated, the less likely you are to garner promotional exposure for your product or service. Certainly reporters know there is an underlying commercial motivation for your helpfulness and everyone understands that is how it works. The problem arises when someone steps beyond this tacit understanding and goes into full advertiser mode.

If you can understand and work with the advertising vs publicity difference you will be light years ahead of your competition. On quite a few occasions we have helped client companies completely outplay their exponentially larger competitors by thinking like a journalist when we approach the media rather than maintaining an advertiser mindset.

There are two simple self tests you can conduct to see if you are on the right side of the advertising/publicity distinction. First, read your press release or media pitch letter to see if it reads like advertising copy. Do you reference your trademarked brand more than twice? Does the piece include too many superlative words? Are your claims a bit grandiose? If your answer is yes to any of these questions, you are doing it wrong and doing yourself a disservice. It is time to change course.

Next there is a second step on this self check and that is to review your personal messaging and typical commentary. Again, does it sound like you are trying to sell something? At one extreme, and we have seen this way to many times, a brand builder in his or her excitement will come off almost like an infomercial pitchman. It kills credibility and turns off reporters in about ten seconds.

While that is the extreme case for illustration, please understand that anything that can be perceived as ad-like will undo even the best prepared fame plans. As with other media pitfalls it is best to err on the side of caution, so we suggest a final step in reviewing your material and media messaging. Run it all by a trusted outsider who you know will give you a true opinion, not limited by concerns of hurting your feelings.

Your competitors, even if they understand the benefits of publicity and are pursuing media attention, very likely do not understand the advertising vs publicity distinction. Get this right and you will not only skip your rookie year, you may well reap the benefits of massive media support. So few people do this properly that when a producer or reporter finds someone with this skill, they will support your efforts in some pretty terrific ways.

WHEN FAME COMES KNOCKING DO NOT BE NAPPING

In Hollywood, on Wall Street, and in power capitals everywhere, the uber successful personal brands know that to make it you must do what it takes. Unfortunately popular culture, fed by films and MTV has corrupted the definition of this fundamental concept. The gangster videos and movies

carry the message that *doing what it takes* means lying, cheating, back stab-
bing, and otherwise sliming your way to the top.

The reality is that unless you're trying to become one of the jailed
CEOs, assassinated drug kingpins or cast-aside waitress/actors, the definition is completely flawed. Doing what it takes, in our world of building
lasting fame, means smart hard work and going the extra mile when your
competition stays home.

We see this regularly in our personal brand management work. It is
really easy to spot the ones who will make it really big and those who will
do only pretty well. The test seems like a small matter at the time but this
is a real life example of the old saying that you can determine the outcome
by its beginning.

Here is an example of what we are talking about. In this book we have
learned that the right media appearance can bump your brand to the head
of the class, typically defined as a leading voice position in your industry
and target market. Your months or years of effort will ultimately result in
one life changing phone call. Your test will be first whether or not you are
there to answer it and second, how you respond.

So here's the call: an editor from a national women's magazine has
heard about your upcoming book, read some of your articles, and one of
her assistants attended your workshop at a conference. You are still a media
unknown but she believes you're worth a try when she has a deadline in 48
hours and the subject of her cover article was just very publicly arrested for
drugs. The editor has three people in mind for a substitute article and you
are number one on the list, but remember you're just one of three.

You are easy to find because you have a contact phone number on your
press releases and your website. The editor is in California and calls Friday
afternoon at 4:15 PM her time. You live on the east coast so it's 7:15 where
you are and you either do not take the call because you don't want to work

after normal business hours or you left your phone at home because "nothing ever really happens after 5:00." Either way the editor gets voice mail.

If she has a 48 hour deadline, and this happens so often that it has become almost the norm, there won't be a voicemail asking you to call her urgently. Rather, because you're still a neophyte brand, she will call her second choice and then the third. Whoever picks up the phone wins a partial cover story in a national women's magazine and one of the largest wins possible for a personal brand.

In this quite-common scenario, doing what it takes means simply being available to receive the results of all your brand building work. You must allow for time zones and the fact that media cycles have absolutely nothing to do with the nine to five world. Further, many editors, producers, reporters, and writers work quirky hours because that is when they are at their best or what their deadline requires.

Until you have built your fame credibility with multiple national media appearances, you simply must be reachable 24 hours a day. If this is too much for you to handle, get a publicist or personal assistant who can take a call, respond to an email, or otherwise capture the opportunity on your behalf. Do what we suggest in this book and you will get that call but you must answer the phone.

That all seems really easy but you would be amazed at how many people have such a high opinion of their brand that they believe they'll get a voice mail in our illustrative scenario. These are the people who have no clue about doing what it takes. They are dooming themselves to a second tier branding position absent a great deal of luck.

The second way we are able to spot people who are destined for success is by their reaction to inconvenient opportunities. Every month there is at least one great opportunity for one of our clients to do a national show but the timing is very short or inopportune. The client may live on the west coast and a morning show needs him to appear the next day for an east coast show. He must be on set, in New York at 3:00 AM for hair and makeup which would require he catch a flight from Los Angeles in two hours. This is all pretty intense the first time it happens but it is exactly the way these things work at least 25% of the time.

There is only one correct answer for a personal brand at the building stage. That answer is an unequivocal and immediate yes. If the kids have to get to soccer, you're hosting a cocktail party that night, your boss needs a report, you have a hot date, or you have the mother of all headaches, those things are important but your answer must be yes to the producer.

Doing what it takes means having the mindset that when an important branding opportunity presents itself, you will always accept. You must develop sufficient confidence in yourself that you know you can handle, in some way, all your other commitments. Another parent can take the kids to the game and keep them for the night. Your husband can cover for you at the cocktail party and anyone would understand your absence for national media. Do your report for the boss on the plane and email the result; what does it matter if you do it in your office or in seat 23B? Headache? It will be gone tomorrow.

If you take one thing from reading FAME 101, this section might be the most important. To become a powerful national brand, you must do what it takes. When you win the fame lottery, which you will, and get the call for a big media opportunity, you must accept no matter what. It's a matter of priorities; on the way up yours must revolve around your brand. Be reachable and be available; your fame awaits.

TO BE A FEATURED EXPERT YOU MUST BE ONE AND STAY ONE

The media is always looking for fresh new experts to comment on the news of the day or on societal trends. When the same experts keep showing up again and again in the same media outlet, the production quality is lessened and so there is a constant search for new notables which creates an opening for an upcoming big personal brand.

Thus a measurable portion of your media efforts, as you have learned elsewhere in FAME 101, will be establishing your credentials and desirability as a subject expert with the media. A former fighter pilot or airline captain can be a great commentator on FAA safety issues. A recent clothing industry executive could be a terrific provider of great content on fashion and a relationship author can be a very valuable source on all manner of subjects.

This is all publicity 101 but there is a mission critical issue underlying the success of this strategy that too many would-be experts simply miss. Anyone who wants to establish expert status in their field must remember that, just as the media is looking for experts, to become one you will need to actually be very knowledgeable on your subject matter and also up to date.

While we are not saying you must have twenty years' experience in the field and have a staff constantly researching new trends in order to qualify as a media worthy expert, you do need three things to be the sort of authority the media will use again and again. The first gating qualification is some experience in the field. Most personal brand builders readily understand this and it is their growing expertise that typically makes them fresh and qualified commentators.

A second characteristic of a mediagenic expert is that they are up to date on the subject. In the above examples, the former airline captain and fighter pilot undoubtedly have a deep base of knowledge but their long-term success will depend on whether or not they have kept up. A pilot from the first Gulf War, without continuous study, will have little qualified commentary on the safety of Boeing's new offering.

Similarly, the fashion industry executive is only partially qualified if his experience was five or even two years ago in this fast-changing industry. The remainder of his qualification will come from study, attending or leading industry events, and perhaps consulting activities which keep him in the day to day flow of the business.

All of this may seem obvious to the outsider but unfortunately when you spend five, ten or even twenty years in an industry you can easily fall in to the trap of believing your expertise to be everlasting without stay-current efforts. So we now get to the final requirement you will need to become a sought-after media expert.

It is this last prerequisite to expert status that trips up so many people because it comes in the form of work. Anyone would think that after 10 years in an industry, your opinion is valuable and you should be able to coast a little because you have a deep understanding of your subject. This is true in most of life but not if you are planning on joining the top one percent of your field.

Just as a doctor, scientist, or attorney will soon become outdated if they fail to keep up on their education, so too will all other possible powerful personal brands. As you have learned in your study of how to get professional fame, you do not need to be the smartest person in your field. You do not need to be the best looking or have the most assets; but you do need to have a current body of knowledge and relevant recent experience.

These are the basic requirements of becoming a media worthy expert. You must stay active and study the field as well as have a basic knowledge of related sectors. For instance, if you head a small restaurant chain you should, in addition to knowing the restaurant industry inside out, understand how the economy affects restaurant patronage, how changing attitudes toward healthy eating affect dining-out decisions, and even how real estate costs are relevant to the success or failure of new and existing retail businesses.

Successful personal brands know that the media is looking for qualified experts who will deliver valuable information to their audience in the form of commentary or sharing new information. Learn your field and stay up to date. Reporters will seek you out and put you in print or on camera again and again.

FAME 101

LEVERAGE FAME

TO JOIN THE LUCRATIVE WORLD OF PROFESSIONAL SPEAKERS

· ·

"Great professional speakers are among the coun try's highest earners and the spin-off benefits are phenomenal. If you can master your Big Speech and market yourself properly, you can easily join this elite group." —Maggie Jessup

· ·

JOIN THE LUCRATIVE WORLD OF PROFESSIONAL SPEAKERS

One of the great benefits you get from investing time, money and energy into branding yourself is that you become eligible to join some of America's highest earners: professional speakers. Everyone knows that former presidents, best-selling authors and other major notables, make hundreds of thousands of dollars each year by giving a small number of talks.

About $75,000 per engagement makes sense for a former Secretary of State and $150,000 seems an okay price to hear 90 minutes of the inside scoop from Bill Clinton, but most of our clients are astounded when they learn that even beginning speakers can make $2,500 to $5,000 for each engagement.

Our research, supported by our clients' experience, shows that any professional can successfully package and market themselves to non profits, associations, corporations, colleges and private groups as a professional speaker. In good economic times or bad, meeting planners have money in their budgets for keynote presenters at their regional, national and international meetings.

There are more than 50,000 events each year where a keynote speaker picks up a fee from $2,500 to $25,000 or more for their 45 to 90 minute presentation. What's really interesting is that only a very limited number of people are pursuing these many opportunities. Why is this? Three reasons come to mind; first, most professionals don't believe they're eligible to be a paid speaker and second, almost everyone who takes a run at getting speaking engagements is held back because they don't know how to get started and finally, of those few who do actually set out to get paid for speaking, most make simple mistakes that prevent them from getting hired and they give up.

The net result of all this is that there is a pool of professional speakers out there, most of whose names you have never heard, who are being paid these great fees 10, 20 or even 50 times a year. What's doubly interesting to us is that when we randomly selected fifty successful speakers and studied their fame platform and personal branding, less than 1 in 5 was even moderately well branded. In fact, some of the field's highest earners have an embarrassingly ineffective online presence, patently self-published books, and offer a generic message supported by few actual qualifications.

All of this is completely unbelievable and yet, absolutely true. There is a very realistic and achievable opportunity for you to add six-figures to your income each and every year. Further, you will quickly outdistance your competitors because you'll see in the next few sections the "secrets" of getting the engagements and you'll be a better pick for the decision makers because you've taken the time to create and package a powerful personal brand.

We know you can do it because we've put quite a number of our clients on the speaking circuit; some were terrified to be in front of an audience when we started with them, others had no idea how many topics they could actually offer as a subject of their keynote, and few had the speech training to create and deliver a compelling message to a large audience. And yet, they're succeeding beyond their own expectations.

Our message here is that wherever you're starting, if you're following the counsel of Fame 101, you can consistently capture paid speaking engagements and you can do this from your very first year in your personal branding process. Could you use an extra $60,000 or even $250,000 each year? Who couldn't? Let's look at the steps you can take right now to put yourself in play.

COURTING THE GATEKEEPERS WHO CONTROL PAID SPEAKING ENGAGEMENTS

There are several steps to winning paid speaking engagements and a number of them must be done simultaneously, but for now we'll separate them and begin with learning who controls these desirable assignments. There are three groups of people you will need to contact who will have the authority to hire you. In fact, most must hire speakers for their organization's or client's events.

Group one is a person, committee or even department inside a company, college or association with the responsibility of putting on events. At a corporate behemoth like NIKE there might be dozens of people spread across worldwide geography with the task of organizing the many training, sales, management, and customer events over the course of a year.

Many of these occasions require keynote speakers, trainers, and/or seminar producers. Large companies spend hundreds of thousands or even millions of dollars each year for these professionals. The downside to the big company speaking engagements is that there is often a complicated process to get qualified as a speaker or presenter and then an equally bureaucratic final selection procedure.

We typically counsel our clients to initially avoid the big companies, large associations or other bureaucracies just because of this tiresome selection process. There is an easier alternative as we discuss below. However, as speakers build their brand and reputation it does become worthwhile to pursue some of the big organizations. An NRA keynote or a training session for the management team of a Fortune 500 company can be insanely profitable.

The second group of people who control paid speaking opportunities is much more accessible and it's these fine folks we recommend you focus on early in your speaking career. A top 20 university will have quite a few people involved in the speaker selection process regardless of the event but a State College likely has just one, or maybe two, people in charge of putting on school events that require speakers. That person is typically quite approachable and is open to solutions.

The same is true of 90% of the thousands of associations in the United States alone; one person or perhaps a small team must find speakers for their monthly, quarterly, annual, local, regional, national and international events. The American Association of Cosmetics Wholesalers, the Oklahoma Association of Small Businesses, and other groups all have a budget for speakers and trainers. These associations might not seem important to you but I promise they are important to their members and group leaders want to find exciting speakers to educate and entertain at events.

Corporations are no different; there are tens of thousands of companies, many with names we've never heard, that hold events for their sales people, their executives and often their customers. The ball bearing industry is huge, as is the metal fabrication, wholesale groceries, children's clothing and firms fitting within hundreds of other categories. So what do wholesale florists and masonry professionals have in common? Companies in their industry have events which require paid speakers; and the best part for you? It's usually just one person who makes the selection.

The third group who can and will be of immense help to your speaking career is an industry unto itself: event planners. Many in-house planners join these few associations but what we're looking at here is those professionals whose career is solely putting on events for client companies, colleges, associations and other groups. What's best is that it's a very small group and if you make a favorable impression on one well-respected member, your reputation will quickly spread and referrals will be numerous.

You can see the idea here: your target group is the people who make decisions about hiring speakers for their events. In our opinion you should initially pursue the profession's low hanging fruit – those organizations with just one easily-accessible decision maker. Your brand and wallet will benefit more from four - $5000 easily-won engagements for somewhat unknown groups than spending a year to capture a $12,000 gig at a prominent group's regional meeting.

CRITICAL ELEMENTS OF AN EFFECTIVE SPEAKER'S MARKETING TOOLKIT

There are a ton of books, DVDs, online courses, seminars, and associations out there, each offering strategies to use as you pursue paid speaking opportunities. Some of their advice is great, some counsel is wrong in our opinion, and other guidance is somewhat suspect as to its effectiveness.

A few of these sources say all you need is a website and to do some cold calling; others insist mailing a simple brochure to event planners is all that's required and still other people suggest a full Hollywood-style eMedia Kit with demo reel is required. While these options cover the entire spectrum of marketing yourself as a speaker, we recommend to our clients and anyone that they follow a combination of these paths.

Why use several marketing options? We absolutely know that the speaking market is such a great opportunity for keynote fees and spin off revenues that it's worth the investment of time and expense up front to maximize the opportunity. So, the question comes down to what do you need and how do you get it out there?

The good news is, if you're following the Fame 101 blueprint, you already have many of the sales tools; in fact, almost all. In our You Dot Com chapter you learn how to create a website to support your personal brand; if you do this, to put your speaking package online you'll only need a Speaking tab and a subpage with its own URL. With this, when you connect on the phone with a booker they'll be able to view your package online while talking. This is one thing that will separate you from the amateurs.

Also with an online speaker page you can add that specific URL to your speaking brochure, demo media, articles you write and every other fame outreach you put in play. A surprising number of opportunities will come your way from an event planner reading an article, spotting you on television, reading your blog or connecting at a book signing. The net message here – use your website to present yourself as a speaker. Make sure your web people include some footage of you onstage at an actual event.

A simple brochure is a must for capturing speaking engagements. It can be as straightforward as a tri-fold but as with everything else we talk about in Fame 101, it must be done by a professional graphics person. That's an easy qualifier for the engagement gatekeepers to spot a professional. We'll talk about content below but for the moment the two reasons you must have a brochure are for direct mail and hard copy follow up.

Direct mail fell out of fashion with the advent of e-communication but Spam has brought it back. For professionals selling high end speaking services, the cost of mailing is justified if your list is great and you'll stand out from the others who are mistakenly sold exclusively on e-marketing. The second reason is you must have a quick standard mailing piece as a follow up to your phone conversations. Many would-be speaking pros miss out at just this stage.

When an event planner asks them to send a package they either spend days racing around trying to put something together, which doesn't work, or they delude themselves into thinking they're in play without the follow-up, or worst case, the potential-hires give the deadly "I don't have one but I'm working on it" amateur response. In all of these cases you've gone from a likely candidate to an extreme long shot. Enough said; get a brochure.

The final piece we suggest is something less than a Hollywood-style media package; at least initially. If you're in the $2,500 to $5,000 fee range, planners don't expect a Diane Sawyer level DVD presentation, but they do want some video with you at an actual presentation. They're looking to see how you interact with the audience. The best planners have learned that people who have great stories and/or are fascinating in person are not necessarily good speakers. They want to see you connecting with the audience.

Some good footage of about five minutes of a presentation goes a long way toward securing your deal. It should include not only some onstage time but also audience shots; one face at a time. For efficiency you can use the same video(s) on your site as you send out in the package.

Again, super quality here is not terribly important until you're at the higher end of the pay scale. If you can film a Rotary luncheon speech with a high quality digital device and ideally have a friend with another one capturing audience reaction, you'll have what you need and what's expected. The important thing is to have it ready to mail or email as a separate file on a moment's notice. Waste a day and they're talking to someone else.

EXPAND YOUR WINS WITH SIZZLING TITLES AND BROADENED SUBJECTS

The gatekeepers to paid speaking engagements are primarily concerned with finding valuable and secondarily, entertaining, content for their audience. Thus, to win an engagement your marketing materials must present the "take away" their audience will receive from your presentation and that take away must be valuable and entertaining. Logical, right? Yes, but your materials must convey what you're offering.

The answer to this is compelling messaging in your marketing package but before looking at that subject we need to bring up a related issue. We see this roadblock in ninety percent of our clients, most of whom become in-demand speakers once we remove it. The barrier we're talking about is too narrow of a focus.

As an example consider the teacher who has studied and written articles on the importance of parental support for the scholastic success of middle school children. This is an interesting subject if I have a son or daughter in middle school or soon to enter seventh grade. There is no doubt this teacher could get some speaking engagements with this specific subject matter and a title reflecting the middle school focus.

However, and here's the thing to note, there are only so many places she will get paid to give her presentation and she'll likely have to travel to hit any big numbers here. Let's look at her skillset and expertise to see how she can geometrically expand her opportunities.

First, she's a teacher; that qualifies her to speak on a variety of subjects. It sounds like she understands middle school kids as well as the parent child relationship. If you have, or have had, a child in 7th or 8th grade you know how rare it is to find someone who understands these transformative years. Further, parents are eager for any information on the subject to survive these often turbulent times.

So, if she has expertise with the kids and if she's studied the student-parent relationship, she likely has some special insights into parents, not just of pre teens but also of the broader subject of parents of school-age children. Expanding that thought she probably has some thoughts on education in general; elementary education preparing kids for middle school, middle school education and preparing students to transition to high school as well as on a variety of public, private, and parochial school issues.

We could rant on further expanding this teacher's brand and speaking expertise but your take away here is to look at your specific expertise beyond what you're doing in your professional activities. No doubt you'll discover scores of subjects on which you have collateral expertise; and the most compelling of these subjects can be offered to event planners as presentations you're qualified and equipped to present.

Many actors understand not only their craft but also the business environment in which that craft is practiced. Political candidates typically focus on a handful of local issues but they usually have in-depth knowledge on one or more of those issues on a national basis. Business leaders are on top of their industry but also have expertise in marketing, supply chain management, finance, human resources and the rest.

Once you've defined your expanded expertise, the content for your brochure, website and the rest will logically follow. Present a strong promise in the titles of your proposed speeches and include four or more offerings rather than just one. We recently heard someone note that if you substitute the word Leadership for Success in your titles or the other way around, it opens all sorts of new doors.

What association, business, or college conference attendees couldn't benefit from new thinking on leadership? At the same time, what audience is not interested in success and the many ways it's defined? The paid speaking engagement gatekeepers, once they are introduced to your marketing materials, are looking for the key words they have in mind; give them a greater chance to find them by presenting offerings well beyond a single-subject message.

LEARN FROM COMEDIANS AND CANDIDATES

It's time for you to create this product you're going to sell for $2,500 or more per event: the Big Speech. We look at creating your messaging elsewhere in this volume; your speech will be an outgrowth of those key messages you develop related to your professional activities. The obvious difference, of course, is that an elevator pitch message is 20 seconds or less and a keynote presentation is typically about 50 minutes. So, this product is different from the messaging.

As a first step in getting you ready for some terrific stage time let's make sure you jump past one of the pitfalls beginning speakers fall into: an unsuitable understanding of the word "speech". For some reason most people think that a speech must be an oratorical phenomenon where one emulates the style of Winston Churchill and that the end product should be an unyielding formal presentation.

Unless you're a political leader, the Pope, or someone of similar position, this is the wrong path. Quite simply you don't want your presentation to be *speechy*. If you follow this simple advice, in every one of your appearances you'll automatically be ahead of 90% of all speakers.

Next comes the hard part; creating your presentation. There is good news and bad news on this subject. The bad news is that you'll likely put in weeks of work to create your Big Speech. This might seem to you to be an insane amount of effort to get ready for a $2,500 presentation to the Association of Harley Davidson Owners regional convention. You're right, under our proposed fame plan for you, it is too much effort for that one event, but it's not just for one event.

You see, the good news dramatically outweighs the bad. You will only need to do this immense effort once. By way of explanation consider the professional life of a comedian. They might be performing in Omaha to-night, El Paso tomorrow and on a Baja cruise ship this next weekend. Do you think they have a different act for each venue? Absolutely not.

How about a candidate for office? They deliver their ideally heartfelt message in town after town and city after city, but it is always the same basic message. This is the beauty in the life of a professional speaker. Once you get your basic message down, which takes some weeks for sure, it can become your base presentation for the next year or two.

It will be new to every audience and so long as you can deliver it with the same enthusiasm that you did on the very first time, you'll get the same positive reaction time after time. Now are we suggesting you give the identical speech, word for word, to the Harley folks as you would the Alabama Association of Retired Executives? Certainly not, however, if you craft your message properly the first time, you will have a base 75% of your content which carries over to almost any audience.

It's likely that messages of freedom, of flexible lifestyle or health would be just a few topics of interest to both of these groups and many more like them. The point is that it's worth the effort to take as long as necessary to create a base speech and then for each engagement you'll only need to put on a customized intro and outro with some group-specific messages included in the body of your remarks.

PREPARATION, PRACTICE, COACHES AND FRIENDS

No one person, with the exception of a handful of superstars in the speech-writing profession, can create a great speech. It is of necessity a collaborative effort filled with rewrites, more rewrites, and then some fine tuning.

In our personal branding practice we advise remarkable and successful people. Almost by definition, even prior to working with us, these folks could stand up and give a quick talk on their subject and they would do quite adequately. Well, if you learn just one thing from Fame 101, make sure to understand that in our world adequate is never good enough if you want to join the top 1% of any field.

The danger is that once you've done several presentations like we reference in the prior paragraph, you might think you're good enough. You might falsely believe that you're that special one who can wing it as a professional speaker and earn the great checks that come with the moniker. We don't care how many of your friends have told you you're fantastic, nor does it matter how many presentations you've done – for our purposes here, you're not ready until you've done your preparation and practice.

Where does this preparation start? Your speech content, whether for a 20 minute presentation or a more formal 50 minute keynote, will always have the same basic structure: Introduction, 3 or 4 core messages, and Outro. Step one will be to prepare a one page outline addressing each of these line items. Take as long as you need to get your structure the way you want it because it will become the foundation of your Big Speech.

Next, spend a week or two or a month if necessary, building the remainder of your content around the basic outline. When you're done go over it several times with the idea of smoothing out any rough edges. In our experience if you actually stand up and read the material aloud, it's easy to spot difficult transitions, awkward phraseology, and places where you get mired down.

You might think you're pretty well done at this point but you're just getting started. Remember the great income that will come to you if you do this properly and you will likely have the enthusiasm to keep going. The next step is to either hire a speech coach or find your friend or associate who is smart as well as brutally honest.

How important is this? We have speech coaches on staff and nearly every client goes through speech training with typically phenomenal results. If your budget doesn't permit the luxury of a professional coach, your professional friend can do nicely. Have them read your speech for content and make comments on what works well, what is okay and what just doesn't measure up.

From here you can refine your presentation and then ask the same friend to listen, without commenting or taking notes, with the intention of commenting on overall effectiveness. This process goes on and on until you have the speech just right. To have some idea of how much time you should invest, consider that when we have a professional coach working with a client, it's typically two hours a week for ten weeks with ample practice and fine tuning between lessons. Overall, a total investment of about three hours per minute of stage time is about right. Remember though, this is how long it takes the first time; thereafter your time commitment is much much less.

What you're looking for is to get to the point where you presentation is So practiced, it seems extemporaneous. When Jerry Seinfeld or the White Trash Comedy Tour guys get up to amuse an audience, every word and the way it's presented is prepared with infinite precision. In fact there are few professionals in any field who put in as much time in perfecting a presentation as do comedians.

As with any profession, to become a well-paid professional speaker you will need to invest the time for practice, coaching, refining and the rest. What will you get out of it? Let's have a look.

HOW LONG IT TAKES TO GET ONSTAGE AND THE NET BENEFIT

Your ability to pick up direct and indirect income from professional speaking is one of the best benefits of building a fame platform. As with the other elements of your effort to create and monetize fame, it will take some time and quite a bit of work but the rewards are nothing short of amazing.

Most or all of our clients at any given time are either preparing to become paid speakers as an element of their professional activities or on the road making it happen and getting better. The thing you must accept is that the "professional" and "paid" elements here do not happen overnight.

As we talk to fame seekers around the country, many have already had some stage time on an unpaid basis. Most have done some business or professional presentations; some have delivered remarks at their Rotary Club or at an industry event, while others have been in the spotlight MC'ing a charity event.

Whether they will fully admit it or not, they've had the addictive thrill of the stage. The actors and bands we work with all already know the feeling and the rush is part of what drew them to their profession. However, for the business person, the early-stage candidate or medical professional, it's new, it's exciting and they want more of it.

The challenge is that because of their modest initial success, e.g., good audience reactions, positive comments afterward or other affirmations, they think they're ready for the stage. All we have to do for them is work out the income aspects. They're rested and ready to pick up a big check; at least in their opinion.

Step one in becoming a professional speaker is to take a realistic look at your present position and to accept that while some of the positive audience reaction was as a result of your stage presence, often times you were being judged as an amateur. We respect and admire anyone with the courage to stand up in front of their peers and give a presentation. After all, the fear of public speaking is greater in many people that the fear of death.

However, you can't even get started until you concede that getting some enthusiastic applause at the local hospital fundraiser is much, much easier than earning a standing ovation from an independent group whose leaders selected you to keynote their event. The difference is quite simply the distinction between being the head of the event committee and being the inspiring author flown in from Austin to deliver a riveting talk on leadership.

Now that we're past the gateway issues, let's jump to the bottom line; what do you get as a professional speaker and how long will it take to earn that title. First, the timing. If you already have a substantial fame platform, you will need only to create your content, work with a coach to develop your presentation and then market yourself to the right decision makers.

This can be done in as little as sixty days although the lead times for hiring paid speakers are a minimum of forty five days and engagements are often set from six months to a year in advance. If you're just getting started building your platform, don't worry; it will only take a few extra months because much of this can be done concurrently with creating your book, your websites and such.

Now what are the rewards of joining this lucrative field? They are many and they are bountiful. First and most obviously you'll get the speaking fee. As we've mentioned elsewhere, they range from $2,500 to $20,000 and more with all travel expenses paid. Note here that you shouldn't set your price below $2,500 because that will brand you as an amateur and you'll miss out on a lot. You can always give a discount if it's an opportunity you really want.

We've shared our opinion that you'll need to write a book. Here is another area where speaking pays off doubly. Your status as a published author will aid immeasurably in winning the engagement in the first place and the additional win is what's called the *back of the room sales.* If your presentation rocks, your audience will want to know more about you and one way to further connect is to buy your book.

In most instances the organization hiring you as a keynote will readily concede to letting you sell your book after the speech. The reality is that the effort is called an Author Signing and someone handles the sale at another table and then buyers come to you with their new book to be signed. It's not unusual to pick up an additional couple of thousand dollars at one event.

In addition to the immediate cash benefits of selling books, there are other valuable benefits to speaking professionally. Possibly the most profitable are the new clients you can attract for your professional activities, the fans you will develop if you're an actor or musician, the votes you'll get if you are a candidate for office, or business opportunities that come from audience members who want to do business with the brilliant author they just heard onstage.

In essence, professional speakers are products. Organizations pay quite a lot for these products and, if you put the time and effort into becoming a truly professional speaker, many audience members will want to "buy" the product. If you're featured onstage with all the related hoopla, it's the same as a Tiffany box or Coach bag; presentation is everything and being onstage increases your value as well as marketability.

We'll see you on the circuit. Fame can be a wonderful thing.

FAME
BARRIERS
THEY ARE
SELF CREATED,
GET PAST THEM

....

"The presence of a celebrity makes any event goo metrically more exciting. Many of your peers won't want you to become that celebrity – you will need to step past their negative voices to gain the spotlight."

—Maggie Jessup

....

YOU HAVE THE FAME FORMULA – WHAT CAN STOP YOU?

If fame is nothing but a formula, why isn't everyone famous? How could you not take advantage of this simple key to an amazing life filled with everything you have ever wanted? Those are great questions and we too are astounded when people who seem to truly want the things fame can give them, fail.

Out of concern that we were missing something, we looked back over the years at all the people we knew who had achieved fame and the many people who failed along the way. We asked ourselves what barrier or barriers were stopping these otherwise high-potential fame seekers from getting to the goal line.

The time we spent on analysis paid off big time; we identified the four barriers that were stopping people on the road to fame. They're really simple and we hope you will take the time to review them because we believe these four obstacles are the only things that can stop you. Understand them, commit them to memory and get past them.

It's interesting to note that the key to getting past the barriers is within your control; these are in no way difficult or impossible to eliminate. We're not talking about not having enough money to achieve fame. We're not talking about not being smart enough, good looking enough or having the right family background or education. The limitations we found are all self imposed.

Here are the four things that can stop you from achieving fame: you expect it to happen too quickly, you don't do what it takes, you try to take shortcuts, or you never actually start. Nothing hard there and yet one or some combination of these knock a substantial percentage of fame seekers out of play and for the rest of their lives they're not really sure what happened. Let's look at each one to make sure this doesn't happen to you.

Want quick fame? Sorry, we can't help you. A properly executed fame plan takes about a year to deliver great results. Sure we've had some clients get lucky breaks along the way and shave a few months off this time period but in our many years of experience we have found it takes a year to start enjoying some good results.

We were even able to identify the time period within that one year, whether our own clients or others we meet on the path, when the highest percentage of people either give up or more likely fade out. This high-risk period takes place between four and eight months following the serious launch of your fame plan.

It's human nature to want to see a reward for doing something and in life the majority of rewards come quickly. Not so with fame. It's hard work and it is surely understandable that after months of steady effort, investing money and taking time away from your family that you would want to see some results.

Unfortunately, building fame is a process of creating a strong foundation and then planting seeds for success. It takes time and many people give up. But for those who stick with it, suddenly they see a break in clouds and they get their first feature newspaper article, they guest on regional television, their book comes out with all the attendant excitement or any of another twenty exciting first rewards. These start happening in the eight to twelve month period following launch. Make it that far and you'll carry forward on the excitement.

Plan for the long haul and accept that you're not The One who can get it done in 90 days. You'll be much happier and more likely to succeed. So what about the other three barriers? Let's look at each one and what it will take to get past them.

THE SHORTCUTS ON THE FAME PATH ARE
PITFALLS IN DISGUISE

If you had the ultimate recipe for the world's best cake and you were a huge cake fan, would you even consider leaving out an ingredient? No, you wouldn't. If you were building a house would you leave out some portion of the foundation? Of course not and yet still many people sabotage their ride to fame by trying to skip past some key element.

As you're learning throughout this book there are several principal elements to the fame formula, each with a number of sub elements. Some are much more fun than others. Working with the media is frequently a thrill but the hours upon hours you spend doing media training can be frustrating and tedious. There is no immediate reward and you even wonder if you're wasting your time because some fame seekers don't believe the media will actually have an interest or they believe they don't have what it takes to stand out in a crowd and deliver a smart message.

Many people love the rush of standing at a podium delivering a keynote speech to an important group of players in their industry; but often these Type A's are the very same ones who can't see the need for practicing one hour for each minute they're to be on that stage. Isn't that simply too much? It's just a speech and perhaps you were on the debate team in college; the need for such deep preparation is for other people.

This story can be told in a hundred different ways: "My message is so interesting I don't need to write a book. Everyone will rush to hear it." "I don't need someone to help with my messaging. I know this subject in extreme detail." You can see the idea and it's natural for people to want to avoid wasting time, but to achieve the kind of fame that will deliver a lifetime of wonderful benefits you must accept there are no shortcuts.

On the difficult road to fame, many seeming shortcuts will appear but each and every one of them is a pitfall in disguise. The fashion consultant will believe he doesn't need wardrobe advice and the veteran newscaster won't accept that his nightly presentation needs some modifications.

Of course that's why the fashion consultant is still at Macy's rather than on their own television show and Katie Couric would still be reading the local news in the boondocks if she didn't listen to outside advice on her presentation – she's been making a mid-seven figure salary for quite a few years now.

You know what? Katie still has an active fame team constantly refining and updating her personal brand. She's smart and she did everything necessary to get to the peak of news fame; she didn't fall for the shortcut trap and neither should you. If Katie Couric announced she was running for Congress, no one would be surprised. If she were selected to run a network, a magazine, or head a national charity, no one would question the decision. That is a powerful personal brand and one she earned.

THE 10 POUND BARRIER

Is it just us or does it seem that everyone in America is going to lose 10 pounds starting first thing next week? You'll see elsewhere in the book that your photo shoot is a key element of fame, even if you're to be a celebrity baker. It amazes me how many people don't start on this early element of their fame plan because they want to wait until they've lost this illusory 10 pounds.

Let's see; on the one hand you can have everything you ever wanted and on the other your cheeks can look a little thinner in your photos. Waiting to pursue fame until your diet begins and finishes is absolute foolishness but a surprisingly frequent barrier on the road to fame. On the other hand, there are some elements that simply cannot move forward until all of the pieces are in place, e.g., your media kit.

If the diet thing were the only crazy barrier for people, we could live with that but unfortunately it is just one of many obstacles that fit in a category: perfectionism. Much of life, and fame too, never happens because people wait until everything is perfect before they get started.

They won't start a new business until they can afford a certain type of computer and when/if the computer gets there they won't get started until a certain kind of software is available and when the new software comes along they need a certain kind of cell phone that can seamlessly merge their contact list. These same people won't sign off on their new website until a never ending stream of requirements is installed…You get the idea.

In order to get somewhere on the fame path, you must actually start. For the perfectionist, which is often merely a label for an excuse or fear of failure, they must accept that nothing will ever be perfect. The timing will never be absolutely right. Sure the kids will be in school in a few months, the new offices will finally be ready, and you'll have the business cards that take six weeks but have that special color you like so much.

If you recognize yourself here and see that perfectionism has been a barrier for you, do this: take out a piece of paper and make a list of four things you can do now, each taking no more than 30 minutes, to move your platform forward. Spend 30 minutes working on your tag line, call someone you find online who does media training, make a list of book titles you'd like to write; anything to get you moving forward. Actually, if you do these several things you're getting ahead on the fame path in three separate areas.

We aren't saying in this section that you shouldn't strive to create the best possible you and keep an eye on the details; all that is important. However, accept that at-best the landscape you're working in will never be more than 90% perfect. That is good enough. Now start building your fame platform and get your photo shoot together; if you actually lose 10 pounds then you can always do another few photos.

SPOTLIGHTPHOBIA OR FEAR OF FAME

Yet another barrier to building a great personal brand, but easy to overcome, is another kind of fear. It's not the fear of success we discussed above; rather it's a fear of having the spotlight on you and being overly concerned about what others think. If you're not ready to step up and step out to become the leading voice of your industry, you'll never achieve fame.

Often the personal challenge is a not-so-subconscious concern that the girl who dumped you in high school (10 years ago!) might see your first television appearance as an expert and you won't be perfect. You're right, you won't be perfect and your second appearance will be better than the first although still not perfect but if you want fame you can't freeze here. And believe me, that girl has probably gained more weight than you, is on her third marriage, just got out of rehab and really doesn't think of you too often. Will you really allow her to stand between you and what fame can deliver to your family?

We often see professionals who are overly concerned about the opinions of every one of their peers. It is impossible to build the kind of unique personal brand that puts you in the top 1 percent of your field without some people finding fault even if that fault is illusory; often because of their own jealousy. In the past year we've seen more than a few people nuke their fame journey by restricting themselves to mediocrity.

In our opinion if someone says "But that's never been done before" or "That's just not how it's done", you're on the right track. It's time to power forward rather than step back to make sure you fit someone else's mold.

The famous break the mold. You're about to step past your peers; do it strategically rather than haphazardly and accept that you'll have a certain amount of detractors.

100% of the time when we're successful at creating a big personal brand or "fame" for a client, there are a small but very vocal group of detractors within the new celebrity's industry; whether dentistry or opera. They say hurtful things, they spread rumors, and because they're really so loud about the whole thing they can cause your confidence to falter. Just know they are jealous of your book deal or the other early benefits of building a powerful fame platform. Don't let them hold you back; that's what they're trying to do.

DOING WHAT IT TAKES

We've looked at several ways to block yourself from achieving fame: trying to shortcut the process, waiting for a 10 pound event, and worrying unnecessarily about the opinions of others. These are all somewhat subconscious self-created barriers but what about the big one? Are you willing to do what it takes to become the icon of your field?

Creating or capturing fame isn't easy; at least not in the first year. It's hard work with no precisely defined reward and few short term results. If you're lazy you won't be famous; it takes consistent long term hard work. Many people fall off the fame path after a terrific several week start but then something comes up.

There is a sick child, a family vacation, a crisis at work, a financial setback or a two-week bout with the flu. Obviously we don't suggest ignoring your responsibilities or your health, but these are the times that separate the ones who will achieve fame and the rest. If you have a sick child you're not sleeping anyway; have a pad and pencil in the sick room so you can be working on the outline for your book.

The vacation? Where better to be inspired to work on your messaging and read up on your industry than at the beach cottage before everyone gets up in the morning? So it all comes down to doing what it takes. We see it in our clients all the time; those that step out of play for a couple of weeks because of the flu – they usually don't make it.

Those that take a day off for the flu but assure us, in a flu-riddled voice, that they will show up for a media opportunity if needed – they pass this early test; we know they're going to make it. So when you set out on your fame path, you might as well decide early whether you're willing to do what it takes. If the answer is No, there is nothing wrong with that; fame isn't for you but don't waste your resources chasing fame in a half hearted manner. You simply won't win.

FOCUS: THE TRAIT OF CHAMPIONS AND SURELY THE FAMOUS

A personal attribute we've identified in 90% of our successful clients and other thriving personal brands we've studied is an uncanny sense of focus. We aren't talking about the ability to fully concentrate on a subject for five minutes but something much more. These people can identify the most important thing to be doing at any given moment and even amidst life's sometimes chaotic existence, they can focus 100% of their attention on that important matter – for as long as it takes.

Think about it. You rarely see the ADD or ADHD types with powerful personal brands. If you look at all the different people whose great brands we use in this book for illustration, you can see they are mostly rock-solid steady. You just know they have incredible focus.

Here's where this ability to concentrate will be most relevant to your situation. At every stage of the fame process there are at least a half dozen random elements of fame needing your attention at any given moment.

You should be working on your book but you need a home run speech by the end of the month. Your website needs attention and someone should be contacting magazines about publishing your article; never mind that you also need to actually write that article.

Your personal fame plan calls for you to put together an association in your industry and consistently pitch radio shows around the country to include you as a guest; and these are just a few of the important fame activities screaming for your attention. You're excited about the fame formula but you can't stop thinking about each and every element.

We have a strategy we call Spidering in the chapter on creating your own personal fame plan but for right here, the important thing is that successful people can push aside all the things competing for their time. They have the ability to focus on just one important subject, in this case a fame element, and do what it takes to move that element forward.

Multitasking can be a bad thing and if you try to do it all and do it at once, you will fail. So open the file and get that article done. You can focus on pitching radio stations later the same day but something has to be completed. The more fame items you can check off your list, the closer you are to fame. Ten unfinished projects won't get it done but five completed important steps forward can be a great thing.

THE FAME KILLERS - NEGATIVE PEOPLE

You absolutely cannot have negative people around you if you want to build a fame platform. The importance of this concept is often underestimated because no single negative comment or action by someone will derail you from the fame path so it's easy to let this one slide. However, the cumulative result of consistent negative messages from one or more people will be a fame killer every time.

What's tough is that sometimes it's difficult to spot the negative person but you must have this talent. We've identified three typical categories of pessimistic and downbeat people so that you can be on the lookout. Building fame, especially in the first year, is hard enough without outsiders suggesting the whole effort is futile.

The first type of downer-person believes that life sucks for everyone and that living is something that must be endured rather than enjoyed. They're easy to spot because when you ask how they are, there is a ready list of job problems, kid crises, and health ailments. A thirty minute conversation is exhausting and you, being polite, feel awkward if you have any great news or expectations to share so you find something wrong in your life to share on that call or at that lunch; and from there starts your downward slide.

You hang up the phone after the negative call and it's next to impossible to get fired up about writing another 500 words in your book or putting in some hours making a media list to contact when your book launches. Get downer-person out of your life or at least minimize the contacts.

Negative type number two believes there are no positive outcomes in life; especially if things are great they readily point out that something bad is on the way. These folks are serious when they say the light at the end of the tunnel is an oncoming train. How can you put in hour number sixty perfecting your speech when this person says "I don't know why you're doing that; no one is going to pay you to speak – that's other people."

In our experience this style of negativity often comes from well meaning, but twisted, relatives. They want to protect you from all the bad things they've seen in their lives and somewhere along the line they have picked up a negative mindset. So by protecting you they are in fact nuking the optimism required to build a fame platform; again, especially in the first year.

So it's your mother in law "protecting you" and you can't really get her out of your life; perhaps an avoidance strategy is best until you've gotten your book deal, given that first big speech or CNN expert appearance. Even then she'll be negative but from that point on it will be hard to derail your enthusiasm.

We've learned to spot this final type of negative person and we promise if you have some measure of success, they'll be around. These are the people with the character flaw of jealousy. Unfortunately we see it all the time with our clients reporting some bizarre behavior from their acquaintances and sometimes family.

Apparently supportive spouses go ballistic when the fame seeker starts getting national media attention. They don't attack directly because that would look petty; rather they attack those things you're doing or the beneficial relationships you're developing that are necessary to maximize your fame. Adult children often do the same with family wrenching results.

On at least several occasions we've had newly successful clients literally beg us to get their children some press, on any subject, because they have become so horrible as mom or dad achieves their dreams. It's the family fame killers who are the hardest to spot; when it's someone else and you see some wackiness you can identify jealousy and not be derailed.

Our message: expect and avoid pessimistic, downbeat and depressing people. It takes courage, stamina, and occasional blind optimism to handle the first year of fame building. You're not getting many rewards and have little to show for the effort during this time so it's easy to be susceptible to negativity, especially from family and friends. So, should you dump everyone? No, just minimize contact or quickly deflect unhelpfulness until your platform is up and operating.

BELIEVING YOUR OWN PRESS

There are many who find a modicum of success on their path to fame and who seriously throw it away by believing their own press and then using the perceived power it conveys against the very people that helped them along the way. No, this isn't a plot to a bad movie, we assure you it happens with remarkable frequency and it always delivers a dismal outcome.

The worst thing you can do is turn on your friends, family, your publicist, or your media friends, all of whom have stood by you, built you up, helped to craft your mediagenic role and built the new and fragile pedestal you are sitting on. These people are home base; they are your safety net. Don't alienate them with an over-inflated ego.

When reporters call to interview you as the expert in your field and offer to keep you on as a source for future stories, don't kid yourself into believing that you have made it. We have actually seen clients divorce their spouse because now that they are 'famous' they think they can and should do much better.

We know this from repeated first hand experience as we've had to dismiss a surprising number of clients who developed what we call the Diva Attitude.

Once you have started to slide down this slippery slope, it is very difficult to get back. The media world is very small; word does get out as to who is difficult to work with and who is a pleasure. Strive to be the latter. And, no matter how much fame and success you garner, there will always be low periods when a strong personal support group is a wonderful safety net.

DUCK THESE BARRIERS

There are so few roadblocks to fame but nearly everyone who tries for fame gets knocked off the path by one or another; it doesn't seem right but that's the way it is. You've seen the list of obstacles now. Is there anything not easily within your control? No, fame is yours if you duck these barriers.

As a final preparation for your effort we want to caution you on three additional things, less than complete barriers along the fame path but still self-caused challenges we have seen slow people down. They are, not necessarily in order of importance: following the latest trend, following your passion, and finally, a poverty attitude. Let's take a quick look at each.

We repeatedly see fame seekers, perhaps four or five months into the year-long effort, want to pursue the latest trend. Maybe it's a new area in aesthetic medicine or a new type of reality TV show; what it is doesn't matter in this illustration as much as our caution to avoid falling for the latest trend. While you might want to stop everything and race to what seems to be working for others… don't.

By the time it's a hot trend and the media is picking up on it – you can't catch it. Further, in our experience as soon as the latest trend gets media attention, so many people jump into it, well the old adage Success Breeds Ruinous Competition kicks in and the latest trend is yesterday's news. Don't fall for the temptation.

A similarly dangerous diversion is when someone decides it's finally time in their life to follow their passion. Authors and speakers who sell the positive thinking pitch always tell you to follow your passion and all else will fall into place. In our opinion this is nonsense and has all the potential in the world to lead you to make horrible decisions.

We believe you should base your fame platform on what you're good at that is marketable. If you write terrific non-fiction material but want to write a novel, okay do it but only after you're on the non-fiction best seller list and then your publisher will probably do a fiction deal for you as a courtesy but knowing, as we do, that it may be your passion but it doesn't have the horsepower to become a commercial success.

The easiest diversion to remedy but one that is potentially fatal to building a successful fame platform is making sure you don't have what many call a poverty attitude. Without getting all New Agey, it is a truth that if you believe you'll be successful in achieving fame, your subconscious goes to work to make it happen.

Conversely, if you focus on what can go wrong, the resources you might not yet have, and the reasons it might not work for you, your subconscious will cause you to fail. Simply have an abundance attitude and it will serve you well. Fame is yours if you want it; we know this because we create it for our clients every day. Almost without exception the formula works for anyone and everyone; accept from our experience that fame is yours if you simply follow that formula and do what it takes.

FAME
FOR LIFE
MAINTAINING YOUR
PERSONAL BRAND

"There is something empowering about walking into a room full of strangers where everyone already knows who you are and they are excited about meeting you. Fame gives you that; every room, every time."
                                                    —Jay Jessup

AVOID THE OVEREXPOSURE TRAP

Tom Hanks and Jodie Foster have had fantastic careers spanning decades and they're still on top of every celebrity chart; they consistently earn eight figures for their films. Movie goers love them both and we are really glad to see them on the morning show circuit; we can't get enough of either one. The reason? They have strategically avoided the overexposure trap. We can learn a valuable lesson from them.

Think back over the years and you'll note there are many B list entertainers who are on talk shows, game shows, and in every magazine every month – year after year. They're often Jimmy Kimmel's warm up guests for when the A listers arrive. What's a big difference between Jodie Foster and the B list? You only see her two or three months a year at the most.

Here's what is going on and for those of you who plan to put what you learn in Fame 101 into action, pay attention. It can be very addictive when you hit the base level of fame and the media is finally seeking you out after months or years of cultivating their attention. You have tried for so long to become a celebrity in your field, one would think it's time to grab all the media you can get for as long as you can get it.

That is the overexposure trap. There comes a point, and we see this in every successful fame launch we orchestrate, when it's time to stop clamoring and start pulling back; strategic quality takes the place of quantity. Overexposure can be illustrated by a visit from your sister in law. You're thrilled to see her once a year, glad to see her twice a year, sometimes troubled to see her monthly and you quickly dread her weekly visits.

We see Jodie and Tom for two or perhaps three months a year and only when they have something to sell. Except for the very occasional high-end interview like Barbara Walters, Charlie Rose, or Larry King, they appear only when a new film is out and we see them in very concentrated doses. They do every talk show and they're on every magazine cover. We hear about their children, their charities, and ultimately their new film or project.

Everyone is interested in Jodie and Tom; we're catching up on what they've been up to. Consider your own family dinner table. Aren't some of the best meals when you haven't been together for a week and everyone has something new to tell? No one fights and everyone is excited to share and to hear.

So too with Jodie and Tom but every time, year after year, they withdraw from the limelight when the film's been launched. They head back to their personal lives to get ready for the next big thing. Their publicity people understand the play and plan for months in advance for high concentrations of media; then nothing.

What does all this have to do with a plastic surgeon in Omaha who wants to maximize his celebrity value? Everything. You've learned he can become a media magnet in about a year; the media and others will seek him out. That is when, to maximize the long term value of his personal brand, he must become strategic in his media appearances.

This isn't to suggest Dr. Omaha should go completely dark like Tom or Jodie, but rather learn to accept only strategic personal appearances and profitable media opportunities. In Year One he might well do a third tier radio several times but in Year Two there is no reason to do that show if the appearance doesn't generate new patients or book sales.

For those of you who work hard enough to get famous, the overexposure trap is tough – it's hard to say no. However, everyone who wants the media and the public to be thrilled to see them for a decade or more should learn from Jodie Foster and Tom Hanks; we'll be thrilled to see you.

MAKING THE CHARITY CONNECTION

What about giving back? Fame will bring you some amazing things and this gives you the power platform to do great charitable things in the world. In fact, we've found charity work to be a common element among the lasting celebrities. Whether it's Angelina Jolie very publicly visiting Darfur to raise awareness of the crisis, husband Brad in New Orleans working on housing for Katrina victims or your local dentist raising money for the town youth center, the lasting brands all lend a hand.

It works both ways too. Do some research and you'll find that the most successful charities have celebrity connections; the locally famous for local causes and the nationally famous for the broader based nonprofits that are doing something big. Both sides of the celebrity – charity equation understand they're benefiting from each other's halo effect and the successful ones seek each other out.

Here's the thing, though; the celebrity must be sincere in their desire to help. This fame element isn't a quick flight to a crisis spot for a photo op – you really must be doing something substantial. When Paris Hilton has a gaggle of paparazzi capturing the image of her hugging an orphan the day before trial following her her umpteenth run-in with the law, her intentions are obvious and it becomes a very negative personal branding moment.

Do you have to become Mother Theresa? No, and none of these cautions suggest that you can't strategically select your charity, publicize your connection and gather the occasional photo or video op. This is one of the beauties of the fame formula; no one will deny you the fame benefits of your charitable actions if you are truly helping out a good cause.

Before we look at how to select the best cause for your personal brand, let's consider the many opportunities where you can capture publicity when you connect with a charity. For example, when Sally Jones decides to go to Darfur, that's a publicizable event worthy of a press release.

The same holds true when Sally reports from Darfur, when Sally returns from Darfur, when Sally speaks out at events for the needs of Darfur's victims, when Sally is organizing shipments of needed supplies to this crisis area, and when those shipments are received by the needy. The publicity benefits of your good work are ongoing but you see what it takes; Sally must actually be doing something on an ongoing basis.

If you are doing something good, it makes sense that you can enjoy the spin off benefits to your personal brand. Photos, videos, and press releases are all suitably in good taste. The big question is how to you pick the charity to connect with? Your selection should be something you emotionally connect with because it will be hard work and that connection will make it much easier for you to do.

The next step is to select among your three choices of charity types: a well-recognized broad national charity, a niche charity which may be local or national, or you can start your own organization. All have their benefits but to maximize your personal potential the second two options are the best unless you are already a major league brand who won't be eclipsed by the charity's own brand.

We rarely see celebrities connect long term with large organizations like United Way. Certainly there are dinners and auctions where celebrities make an appearance, but in our experience the bureaucracy of the United Way and some others does not permit any significant sharing of the limelight. A charity is a business, albeit technically in IRS terms a non profit, and the highly compensated leaders are working on their brands too.

A better choice, whatever your field, will be a locally grown charity where your co-branding can make a measurable and mediagenic difference, or a niche national charity, with a single message or mission, where your leadership will be most needed. As you deal with the leaders of these organizations you're often connecting with one or two people rather than an unseen committee. This personal connection can be the basis for a long-term beneficial relationship: to you, to the organization and of course to the people it serves.

The final choice is a much bigger commitment but one you might consider. You can start your own effort, whether it be a one-time rescue effort to get the victims of a disaster back on their feet, or a longer term established 501c3 charity that you would run exactly like any other business but the revenues come from donations or grants.

Accept that a common element of long lasting fame is a strong reciprocally beneficial charity connection. Find yours, connect, and do something. Share the halo effect of your fame and join the ranks of Celebrities Doing Good.

THE NICE PEOPLE AT DEATH KILLER RECORDS

You wouldn't expect the executives at Death Killer Records to be among the nicest people in the entertainment industry. They don't want to be known for this because it would kill their image, and this is why we're using a fictitious name, but these bling'd out gangstas will lend a hand or their checkbook to any worthy cause. They take care of their kids and step up when charity comes calling.

If the concept of rap philanthropy amazes you, it shouldn't. The common element we found among every lasting celebrity, which would include these guys with a decade of success in a murderously competitive industry, is that they are just plain nice. The outward façade is simply costuming and great branding.

We see this all the time when we introduce people to some of our more lastingly famous clients in informal situations. Almost without exception people say "Wow, he is just a regular guy – not at all what I expected." And that is exactly what you want regardless of your fame sector. It applies just as much to the celebrity dentist as it does to Jennifer Aniston who by the way is really, really nice.

We learned this from studying successful political campaigns. It's why candidates drive around Kansas shaking hands, eating barbeque and doing photo ops with the local scout troop. In the fame world, every time you connect personally and that person likes you, you have a walking advertisement. People will talk for years about shaking hands with a candidate, a kind word from a B-list entertainer or meeting the celebrity dentist who is in the local newspaper all the time.

It just pays to be nice. Connect on a positive note with just a hundred people and ten thousand will ultimately hear about how nice you are; people talk. Is it necessary to be amazingly charismatic? No, you only need to acknowledge them in a positive manner and not be seen as putting on airs.

One technique you can use to further enhance your likeability quotient though is going one step beyond nice. By this we mean being interested; interested in the people you connect with. All of us like to talk about what's important in our lives. Our kids, our jobs, our hobbies or even our thoughts on the economy. Don't talk about yourself; talk about the people you're meeting. Leave a lasting impression for lasting fame.

If you do this authentically, i.e., your interest must be real because people have a built in phony-meter, pretty much everyone will like you and tell everyone they know. President Bill Clinton has this talent. Not just when campaigning, but also during his presidency and even now he connects quickly with everyone he meets. His schedule often only permits him to speak with someone for just a minute or two; but during this period, as far as Bill is concerned, there is no one in the world more important than that person.

What can we learn from this popular president and others? The long lasting celebrities do not have self esteem issues where they must pontificate and monopolize every conversation. The most loved celebrities are those who listen and are truly interested in the lives of everyone they meet. And of course, they are truly nice. If you do this, you'll develop a fan base (yes, dentists, gardeners and teachers can have a fan base) that will help you achieve your every goal.

CONSTANT FORWARD MOTION – MAINTAINING PERSONAL BRAND MOMENTUM

Can you name a dozen personal brands who captured the spotlight and then faded away after one or two years or even after six months? These are the one hit wonders, the one book wonders, or even the very visible association president who fell into obscurity after a brief connection with fame. We have people come to us all the time to re-launch their brand; almost all unaware of why their initial celebrity evaporated.

On the other hand there are people on whom the spotlight stays year after year. What's the difference between the long lasting personal brands and the rest? The best players focus constantly on personal brand momentum and if you're building a lifelong personal brand, you must pay attention.

We can learn a lot from brand master Donald Trump. Over the past 15 years not a month has gone by without the Donald's brand being Trumpeted in the media. Expensive divorces, trophy marriages, a well-branded daughter, big wealth, epic debt, casinos, magazines, big hair, Trump books, Trump Towers, Trump University, The Donald action figures, and even a reality show based on his search for an assistant – a brand momentum machine.

Here's the lesson: when the fame machine clicks in for you and you're busier than ever with appearances, books, new business opportunities and yes, the parties, it is very easy to believe you've made it and that for the rest of your life your brand will carry you forward. It certainly can but only if, no matter how busy you become, you maintain the brand with constant forward motion.

Copy Trump's strategy; you must have a one year rolling marketing and publicity plan with proactive brand building activities every single month, if not every week. This counsel might seem in conflict with our advice to avoid overexposure but nothing could be farther from the truth. Nine months ahead you might be planning the book tour for the volume you haven't started yet.

The very same strategy applies to everyday celebrities too. Authors should be seeking reviews, radio shows and working on their next book every single day. The celebrity dentist should be learning the business side of practicing dentistry, particularly the collateral businesses that operate around the profession, e.g., what companies are producing the next generation equipment or materials and how to connect with them.

Put a post it note on your computer, your refrigerator or bathroom mirror that reads Constant Forward Motion. Whoever said centuries ago that a journey of a thousand miles begins with just one step probably never imagined the importance of the concept in branding in the 21st century but they were right. Make sure you, or someone on your behalf, is making daily efforts to advance your brand. The cumulative results are powerful and the constant forward motion is critical to maintaining a Powerful Personal Brand – for life.

BUILD YOUR NETWORK, BUT DON'T NETWORK

We can say with absolute certainty that every single one of your opportunities will come from a person or a small group of people directed by just one person. It may be the decision maker at a non-fiction publisher, a producer at a Miami television station, one person who is the head of the speakers' committee for an annual industry convention, the head of a state political party or anyone else who decides which person to plug into an opportunity.

If you accept this premise then your strategy for creating a big brand is to connect with many such people in a positive way. Obviously this can't happen while you're sitting at home so it is important that you consistently get out and about to events or meetings where people who can help you are found.

Most business people especially understand this concept but they only get half of the message. Almost everyone has been to their industry convention, meetings and conferences designed to connect people while presenting the latest and greatest in services to support the industry. If you're diligently attending such events you're connecting with people who can help you but you're missing the bigger opportunity.

The real stars of business or any other sector know that you must expand your personal network beyond your own industry. For instance, if you're a lawyer you go to legal events; the smarter lawyers also get involved in the activities of their subspecialties but the celebrity lawyers go where the prospective clients are and where members of the media are visible on a social basis. Ultimately they use their platforms to secure keynote spots in front of these audiences.

By way of example consider the business attorney who speaks at the regional medical association conference on the subject of enhancing profitability in medical practices. Who do you think they will call when it's time to get new counsel and profits are down? Or consider the plastic surgeon who keynotes at the monthly Republican Women's luncheon on reversing the effects of gravity and age.

The formula is no different for entertainers going out beyond film industry events and connecting at places where there are new fans, members of the media are congregating on a social basis, or even appearing at that same legal conference. As you rise to the top with your brand, it becomes more and more important to build your network outside of your industry.

There is one admonition here. The title of this section reads also "Don't network"; this flies in the face of every $20 book on success but you won't get past the lower rungs on the fame ladder unless you absolutely understand the distinction between networking and building your network. Remember: Networking Bad, Building your Network – Good. But, is this inconsistent?

No, the idea is best illustrated by example. At the end of a small business trade show day, two young lawyers are having a sandwich and discussing what business development activities they had accomplished. One proudly displays thirty business cards he collected with personal notes detailing the contact written on each. It was exactly as if he was keeping score by the quantity of contacts.

The other lawyer, the one with fame potential because he understands the importance of building a network rather than networking, explains he met just three people. This fame candidate understands that quality is much more important than quantity as you build your network.

He sought out three people who he knew in advance would be there and spoke with them on a personal basis; nothing about "What can you do for me now?" but rather "Is there any way we might work together over the long run?" as well as taking the time to get to know these three people.

Powerful personal brands understand the importance and value of just one key relationship. In building your personal brand, constantly be aware of the balance between pushing too fast and the value of building a long term relationship. So, if you meet a television producer who is doing a special next week on your area of expertise, it's okay to pitch hard and fast. If it's a television producer who does a health show every week, take the longer view.

What are the lessons here? Make long term business relationships inside and outside your industry. And, don't visibly network. Do you ever see a famous person working the room? Absolutely not; the room comes to them. Fame is being that person.

HELP MEDIA FRIENDS

Last week we were at a charity auction here in Portland. It's a brilliantly produced annual event where everyone has a blast while raising money for an important local non profit. Among the guests were a handful of people from the Oregonian as well as from both local television stations.

We were in a small group talking to a business reporter when a business woman with a bit of a reputation for having an unduly high opinion of herself joined the conversation. Within a minute she had shifted the conversation from our upcoming Rose Festival to micro details of a new product line she was taking on in her not-very-interesting industry.

She was speaking directly to the reporter as if none of the rest of us were even there. After her two minute pitch she said to the reporter "You should do a story on me". Then silence; it felt as if we'd just witnessed a time share sales close. The reporter, accustomed to this sort of intrusion, quickly finessed away from the group.

The woman then told us that she didn't think the reporter was very good because it was obvious he didn't recognize a great story when he saw one. Hopefully you're cringing as you read this story because that shows you understand why this woman has never, and will never, hit the top circle of fame in our community.

People who work in the media have a special celebrity power of their own that often brings out the worst in the attention-seeking public. Anyone in the media is indeed powerful and can do great things for your personal brand but for some reason the never-to-be famous don't seem to understand that these are people and that rules of civilized behavior apply.

At the opposite end of the spectrum from this story are the people with truly lasting brands; brands that consistently bring them great things including positive media attention. As you know, these powerful personal brands are consistently nice and they're nice to everyone, definitely not just to people who can help them.

Lasting brands understand that friends in the media are one element of their success and they indeed cultivate those relationships but on a long term basis. They act like friends should; they keep their eyes out for story opportunities that would help a reporter or producer – almost never having to do with themselves. An experienced reporter can spot a story in a heartbeat; all you need to do is keep them up to date on your activities. When there's a story, they will tell it.

Reporters and producers are judged by the quality of information they deliver to their audiences; if you help them in their careers, most will help you in yours. We'll talk more about this in the chapter on publicity but for now your takeaway from this chapter should be to connect with media people whenever you can but always treat them as you would a friend. Help them along.

PARTING
WORDS

You have the formula for an amazing life and career based on the success blueprint we developed from the strategies of America's elite. You understand that fame, celebrity, and powerful personal branding are all the very same thing. Ideally you also recognize that anyone can create and leverage fame to become one of the privileged and influential people who live in a world of broader opportunities.

Now it is your turn. If you are an author, it's time to do what it takes to sell a million books and maybe get a movie deal or use your author status to create high-income collateral activities. Or perhaps you are a citizen running for office; well now you have the powerful tools used by winning candidates. Declare your candidacy – you have the edge.

Are you an attorney? Use the Fame 101 strategies to attract high-value clients starting today. Whether you are an actor, doctor, real estate broker, or a baker; every one of you can become the next big thing in your field. You can win the big parts, create a massive inflow of new patients, do the big deals, or bake your biscuits on your own television show.

One of the most rewarding aspects of our publicity and personal branding consultancy is we get to see clients have that moment of clarity and vision when they suddenly put all the pieces together and see that fame is a formula. They see how Martha Stewart grew an empire, why John Travolta gets eight figure movie deals, how presidents get elected, and exactly how the notables of their own profession rose to leading voice positions.

Fame 101 puts unlimited professional success at your doorstep. If you have the courage and diligence to step beyond the norm, you can create for yourself an extraordinary life. There is a spot waiting for you at the peak of your profession and among society's elite – go take it.

ABOUT THE AUTHORS

Jay Jessup and Maggie Jessup create and manage Alpha Celebrities in every field with a radical mix of publicity, personal brand strategy, and Brand-You marketing. Their study of publicity and branding secrets of 100 notables including Martha Stewart, Mother Theresa, Pablo Picasso, John Kennedy, Billy Graham, John Grisham, John Travolta, and others led to their Fame Formula which they use to catapult their clients to the top one percent of their professions.

They work with elite professionals, best selling authors, celebrity scientists, high trajectory actors, entrepreneurial royals, leaders of important causes, rock star politicians, startup gurus, breakout bands, very visible artists, and other remarkable people who want to harness the power of a compelling personal brand.

Their clients appear regularly on CNN, MSNBC, Fox & Friends, Air America, ABC News, the Today Show, Good Morning America, and most other outlets as well as in the pages of People, Forbes, InTouch Weekly, USA Today, and scores of similarly varied publications.

Maggie Jessup is a former investigative journalist for the Atlanta Journal Constitution and Houston Chronicle. She co-founded Platform Strategy, a boutique publicity and brand strategy firm where she leads a team of publicists, social media gurus, web technology experts, graphic artists, publishing professionals, media & speech trainers, and marketing people focused on building and managing compelling brands.

Jay Jessup is a leading figure in the personal and corporate brand strategy fields. He speaks frequently at business and professional events ranging from Mensa national conferences to trade association gatherings. His clients are a Who's Who and Who's Next list of high-earning professionals, winning candidates, innovative visionaries, and leaders in varied sectors.

Prior to co-founding Platform Strategy he was chief marketing officer for two hyper growth technology firms and earlier was a rainmaker for national global professional services firms working in the publishing, communication, and entertainment sectors.

Jay and Maggie's pioneering work in personal brand strategy has made them the most recognized experts in the field and among the country's most in-demand branding advisors and speakers.

To contact the authors: www.platformstrategy.com